**William MacQuitty during production of
'A Night to Remember' in 1957**

Film-maker, writer and photographer,
William MacQuitty was born in Belfast,
Northern Ireland in 1905. He lives in London.

D1471015

Also by William MacQuitty

As author and photographer:

Abu Simbel (foreword by I.E.S. Edwards, 1965)

Buddha (foreword by the Dalai Lama, 1969)

Tutankhamun: The Last Journey (1972)

The World in Focus (foreword by Arthur C. Clarke, 1974)

Island of Isis (1976)

The Joy of Knowledge/Random House Encyclopedia
(major contributor, 1977)

The Wisdom of the Ancient Egyptians (1978)

Ramesses the Great, Master of the World (1979)

A Life to Remember (1991)

As photographer:

Irish Gardens with Edward Hyams (1965)

Great Botanical Gardens of the World
with Edward Hyams (1969)

Persia, the Immortal Kingdom
with texts by Roman Girshman, Vladimir Minorsky
and Ramesh Sanghvi (1971)

Princes of Jade with Edmund Capon (1973)

Inside China with Malcolm MacDonald (1980)

The Glory of India with commentary by Chandra Kumar
(foreword by John Masters, 1965)

William MacQuitty

SURVIVAL KIT

How to Reach Ninety and Make the Most of It

with a Preface by
ARTHUR C. CLARKE

Q

Quartet Books

First published by Quartet Books Limited in 1996
A member of the Namara Group
27 Goodge Street
London W1P 2LD

A catalogue record of this book is available from the
British Library

ISBN 0 7043 8014 5

Printed and bound in Finland by WSOY

Quartet gratefully acknowledge permission to quote from
the works listed below: Human Agression by Anthony
Storr, Routledge. Profiles of the Future by Arthur
C.Clarke, Macmillan Publishing Group. All About Strokes
by Alan Bonham Carter, Nelson. Four Quartets by T.S.
Eliot, Faber & Faber Ltd. Proud Songsters by Thomas
Hardy, Macmillan Publishing Group. The Explorer by
Rudyard Kipling, A.P.Watt on behalf of The National
Trust and The Society of Authors as the litereary
representative of the estate of James Stephens.

To People of Goodwill

When William MacQuitty published his autobiography, *A Life To Remember*, to much acclaim in 1991, he was more than halfway through his eighties. The book brought him a flow of questions from readers and the people he met: how had he managed to do such a variety of things in one lifetime and to maintain such a sharp memory of them all?

This is his reply, written from the viewpoint of his nineties. It encapsulates his philosophy and attitude to life, his endless curiosity and his capacity for enjoyment. In considering the facts and meanings of faith and science, of love and friendship, he encourages readers to think for themselves about the questions raised.

Today, as never before, we need to be open, flexible and questioning to all matters of 'received wisdom'. Only thus can we develop positive, creative attitudes to the shortcomings of educational systems, to our chances and opportunities, to the uses of leisure and the artificial expectations of enforced retirement, and ultimately to death, which contains the measure of our lives.

In a world of increasingly ruthless and dangerous ethnic sectarian divisions, William MacQuitty's voice stands out in its warmth, sanity and tolerance. He has written, as Arthur C. Clarke says in his preface, 'a book distilling the wisdom of a lifetime. I recommend it to old and young alike.'

Contents

Acknowledgements

It was the Chartered Bank of India, Australia and China, now the Standard Chartered Bank, that gave me the foundation for all that followed in my life from the time when it took me on its foreign service in 1924. Those years in the Orient, from then until 1939, put me in touch with many of the realities of the world, its beauty, its delights, its horrors. Such experiences helped me to develop a philosophy of life as well as views on how the individual may best enhance whatever deal he or she is handed by fate or destiny and the overwhelming need of the world for sectarian and ethnic tolerance. There was always a tradition in the Chartered Bank to allow strongly individual talents to flourish that went side by side with its integrity in dealing with the exotic peoples it served. To the Chartered Bank I therefore offer my first and profoundest thanks.

My old friend Arthur C. Clarke has greatly encouraged me with the present book, as he has with so many of my past literary endeavours. For this, and for his kindness in providing a Foreword, he has my eternal gratitude.

I am grateful, too, to Peter Ford for an association that goes back almost thirty years to when he took my book *Buddha* under his guiding editorial wing. The present text has once again benefited considerably from his sympathetic editing and many suggestions.

My warm thanks and appreciation go as well to Naim Attallah for having the faith to publish a further book by me. To Jeremy Beale, managing director of Quartet Books, I am likewise grateful for advice and help in overseeing the book from the start of the publishing process; finally I must thank the staff of Quartet Books for dealing so efficiently with all the intricacies arising out of that process.

Preface

I am delighted to contribute this preface to the latest book by my ever-young friend Bill MacQuitty, which he has written to celebrate his ninetieth birthday – especially as I can claim some small credit for starting him on his literary career. His fascinating autobiography, *A Life to Remember*, gives details of our various encounters, and amply demonstrates his unique qualifications for writing this 'Survival Kit'.

Since publishing *Abu Simbel* in 1965, Bill has produced almost a book a year – often very massive volumes indeed, on a remarkable variety of subjects, and with the assistance of the best authorities. The Dalai Lama wrote the introduction to *Buddha* (1969), and in 1971 the Shah of Iran sponsored a beautiful volume to commemorate the 2,500th anniversary of his country. The title may now seem a trifle ironic: *Persia; the Immortal Kingdom*.

Inside China (1980) and *The Glory of India* (1982) would have been enough to occupy an ordinary writer for a couple of lifetimes. Bill must be one of the very few men still with us who can recall at first hand the India of Kipling; for six years in the 1920s he was a volunteer in the Punjab Light Horse, trying to keep peace in Amritsar.

Perhaps the most successful of Bill's books is *Tutankhamun: The Last Journey*, which sold a quarter of a million copies. His haunting photograph of the funerary mask was seen all over the world, as it was used as a poster for the 1972 exhibition of the tomb's treasures.

During the course of his career Bill became a first-class photographer and accumulated over a quarter of a million photographs – all neatly listed and filed in the MacQuitty International Collection. In 1974 he put the best of these together in *The World in Focus*, and I was honoured to write the foreword.

One of the most remarkable aspects of Bill's personality is the way these individual initiatives have gone side by side with his great creative gift for promoting team-work in others. It was illustrated vividly when he combined his profound interest in the civilization of Ancient Egypt with inspiring and developing the British plan to save the temples of Abu Simbel from the rising waters of the Aswan Dam. Later he founded Ulster Television, and created a link with The Queen's University, Belfast, to produce a programme called 'Midnight Oil'. This was a pioneer adult education programme and a direct forerunner for the approach adopted by the Open University.

It is, however, as a film producer that Bill made the greatest impact on the world. His masterpiece for the cinema, *A Night to Remember*, remains unchallenged as the definitive account of the most famous of marine disasters. The dedication of my novel, *The Ghost from the Grand Banks* (1990), is my own tribute to the film:

For my old friend Bill MacQuitty –
who, as a boy,
witnessed the launch of RMS *Titanic*,
and, forty-five years later,
sank her for the second time

And now, eighty-three years later, Bill has written a book distilling the wisdom of a lifetime. I recommend it to young and old alike.

Colombo,   ARTHUR C. CLARKE
Sri Lanka
25 June 1995

SURVIVAL KIT

How to Reach Ninety
and Make the Most of It

Introduction

During my life I have learnt about the importance of living from a handful of people who were wise rather than clever. They were neither rich nor powerful, but they were generous with their wisdom. I learnt from them gradually, over many years, and this small book is a distillation of what they taught me. It is written for anyone who feels they would like to enjoy as fully as possible the rewarding world in which we have the good fortune to live.

Many people today have doubts about much of the received wisdom they were born into or have been expected to accept. Their schooling may have done little to enable them to lead zestful and enjoyable lives. Too many teachers reduce the fascination of the world to a routine of learning often uninteresting information to enable their pupils to pass examination papers that are less than stimulating.

Nothing of the excitement and beauty, the power and the glory of nature was ever discussed in my education three quarters of a century ago. The boys in my Belfast school were placed as if on railway lines, and in the opinion of the teachers these would, if carefully followed, lead to termini of importance. The problem was that, with the senses focused on a final high position, there was no time left over for actually getting off the train every now and then – not even for a brief look at the marvels that lay alongside the tracks on its route.

I therefore experienced an educational system which failed to teach that ambitions for security and indispensability are delusions, that the winners are likely to become the richest men in the cemetery or, heaped with honours, goldfish in a public bowl, their every move eagerly reported by the media. Neither did it teach that all power tends to corrupt and that absolute power corrupts absolutely.

This account of my own way of travelling along the paths of consciousness is a garnering of ideas from people and books – books that became significant to me not because they were recommended reading by experts but because I felt drawn to them. It is a random harvest of responses, a dropping of hints on possible attitudes of mind to be cultivated. My hope is that kindred souls may find it helpful. It aims to provide guidelines to encourage those who wish to lead a full and happy life all the way through to old age, and to enable them to judge for themselves the true value of the innumerable books on these matters. It also explains how, in my nineties, I continue to enjoy life and the marvels of our modern world.

Older people may be daunted by tackling the business of living. Often they feel afraid and descend into ever more lonely lives as their friends die and they fail to replenish them. Younger people are also subject to fear, this tending to centre on their insecurity and a shortage of opportunities in the workplace. They have been brought up to expect that the state will either provide them with jobs, or, if it fails to do so, then will give them money on which to live. This is an unrewarding situation. Inevitably it leads to a lack of personal pride and a feeling of being unwanted. Fortunately remedies do exist, but these depend on adjusting the original expectations considerably.

In my youth it was necessary to depend on oneself – the person in the world who, after all, has the most interest in seeing the development of a satisfactory basis for life. We never expected anyone to help us, apart from our families and friends. Self-help was paramount. Five million people worked in service. Today nannies (the Princess of Wales was at one time a nanny), housekeepers, nurses and baby minders still do, and get well paid for it. Gardeners, window-cleaners, handymen, night-watchmen and home helps always seem to be in short supply. Such jobs should never be turned down as unsuitable or beneath personal dignity. They will enable some among the unemployed to discover themselves and help them to find their true vocation. The great American novelist William Faulkner began his writing life working nights as a boiler man, and there is nothing wrong with cleaning windows so long as you make a good job of it.

There is no obstacle in the way of enterprising young people, so long as they are fit and capable, setting out to work their passage round the world. In many ways, it is easier to do today than it was in the past. Once they cut free from the idea that their lives depend on state security, they can dip their toes in the waters of reality and discover great enjoyment in any job, however humble it may be. The beauty and reward of travel is, for those who can manage it, the broadening of their minds and the discovery that perhaps another country will suit their talents or personalities more than their homeland. Any job has the potential to lead on to a realization of what suits one best. Work is the greatest joy in life, so long as we treat it as an aspect of self-discovery. To find the right path, we need to test out different kinds of work and types of challenge. Our gift may be for working with other people in group enterprises or the caring services; or it may be for something more solitary, involving an individual effort. Some people may take years to find their true vocations, but others, such as musicians or sportsmen, have little time to spare and must lay the foundations as early as possible. It is never too soon to begin tuning in to the inner voice that will be our best guide.

A good simile for getting started in life is learning how to swim. Originally we came from the sea, and small babies love water. Then, when they become a little older, it begins to frighten them, with good reason. Every year hundreds of youngsters drown — terrible ends to young lives. The place to start is in the shallow water, where you can still touch the bottom with your hands as you lie in the water. If you go straight in waist deep, you may not be able to keep your feet on the bottom; your head may go under, causing you to panic and then to need assistance. There will also be an unnecessary loss of confidence. It is best to remain in the shallows until you have mastered the knack of staying afloat. Once you find that you can stay afloat even when you lift your hands from the bottom, then your confidence will be reinforced dramatically. The way will be open for you to try all manner of other actions and activities in the water, from the breast-stroke and crawl to diving and water-skiing.

Examine anything that you find unfamiliar in this book with the same spirit. Take it slowly; suck it and see; try it for yourself. Beware of received wisdom; work out your own salvation. Read what appeals to you. Develop your own ideas of what is best for you. In all your pursuits, you are the one who should be in charge. Discuss everything with your friends, but do not let others decide for you and, at the end of the day, trust yourself. It is sheer laziness to trust others unless they have passed your most stringent scrutiny. You are unique; it is *your* life.

It has been suggested to me that I ought to include

examples of what to do in different situations, but this would fill an encyclopaedia and I have not set out to write a handbook. Each person has his or her own special problems and these must be solved personally. In the United States there are many, including Presidents, who employ psychoanalysts to guide them in their everyday lives. Not only is this very expensive, but it may not be in the best interests of the subject. If psychoanalysts were so knowledgeable, they would be occupying all the top jobs. Close friends may prove to be more helpful than psychoanalysts - or, indeed, astrologers – when it comes to talking things over before reaching your own decisions.

In the new age of automation and computers, machines have already soaked up millions of manual and clerical jobs. Automobiles, like many other machines, are no longer hand-made. Instead they are assembled by automation. Bank passbooks are no longer written up by bank clerks, but are checked and printed off by computers. Secure 'jobs for life' are rapidly vanishing. On the other hand, although the loss of a job may be daunting for those who experience it, it can also provide an opportunity for trying something new and may eventually open a door on to a fresh enjoyment of living.

It may well be better in the future not to set so much store by the so-called 'secure' jobs, like those provided by banking, insurance and other large companies. These are no longer jobs for life, and it could be better anyway to work for oneself, forming one's own little company and hiring out a speciality to the big companies. This then has the attraction for large organizations that they do not need to worry about paying national insurance or pension contributions, or becoming involved in sacking or union problems. Today television and radio companies commission many of their programmes from small outside producers. In Britain the very successful independent Channel Four has no studios of its own, but farms out all its programmes to independent production companies. If you are your own boss, you will work much harder, and for longer hours, but you are also likely to have more fun. In short, anyone is likely to be happier, paddling their own canoe.

I was reared in Northern Ireland, a province of evangelists. The lesson I learnt from them was that those who believe they are unconditionally right are capable of any ruthless outrage and must therefore be wrong in the context of eternity. Orthodox belief is invariably a crippling of the spirit. The true mystic is never afraid of crossing boundaries, and sectarianism is a reductionist negative trend. Today we must have faith in our wider heritage, since we have the same ancestors in common – human beings who were able to survive in the most alarming and dangerous circumstances. Without them we would not be here. No wonder the oldest race in the world, the Chinese, are ancestor worshippers.

Like the great majority of people, I was brought up to believe that mind, soul or spirit, or whatever it might be termed, was God-given and something that existed independently of my body. Somehow this mysterious part of me would survive my body's death. In time I came to doubt it. My God-given brain turned out to be too humble to believe that I had a right to be immortal above the rest of God's creatures, who were said not to be. As one of the great travellers of the age, Wilfred Thesiger, remarked when interviewed by Naim Attallah in the *Oldie* magazine, 27 May 1994: 'I find it very difficult to believe in a God or in an afterlife. I can't see why we're any more important than the ant.'

As the late Professor Joad would have commented, it all depends on what we mean by 'God' or 'the soul'. Science and knowledge have been moving ahead so fast as to leave traditional beliefs floundering amid contradictions, their moral authority steadily eroded. 'Once it was believed that a vital force lay behind all living things,' Professor Lewis

Wolpert has said, speaking as an expert in medical biology. 'Today it is clear that there is nothing but complicated chemistry.' Professor Francis Crick, the co-discoverer with James Watson of the structure of DNA forty years ago, offered a similar view at the *Times*/Dillons Science Forum on 25 May 1994. 'You, your joys, your sorrows and your sense of personal identity are no more than a complex assembly of nerve cells.' But he saw no need to worry that all this future knowledge would reduce our perception of ourselves. 'It will reveal the wonderful complexity of our brains, so that what we lose in mystery we shall gain in awe.'

At the end of the day the mystery will always remain. The facts are as follows. In a lifetime the average person consumes fifty tons of food and 11,000 gallons of liquid, from which we assimilate what our bodies need. The remaining factor essential to health is the oxygen we breathe. Our 10,000 taste buds, aided by 13,000 million nerve cells, help us to choose what we like to eat. The average human being contains enough carbon to equal twenty-eight pounds of coke, enough lime to whitewash a small shed, enough fat to mould seven cakes of soap, enough phosphorous to make the heads for 2,200 matches, as much iron as there is in a one-inch nail. It took more than 3,000 million years of evolution to produce early man, but our cave-dwelling ancestors themselves evolved rapidly during the past 10,000 years to bring us to the point where we are using our five senses and wonderful brain to explore and question the universe. Nevertheless, as the scientist Stephen Hawking has said, 'Science may solve the problem of how the universe began but it cannot answer the question: why does the universe bother to exist?' As the guru I met in India remarked, following along the same tack, 'It is impossible to know the unknowable.'

It seems that the mysterious neurons that compose the physical basis of the mind add up to a kind of sixth sense, capable of being influenced by suggestion and auto-suggestion. Hence it is not difficult to appreciate the power of religion and of demagogic leaders. The atrocities of war and and dictators are supported by the minds of people who abandon common sense and charity. In spite of our endeavours for peace, no less than thirty-seven wars rage around the world at the time of writing, and there may well be worse to follow. In the distant future, when our awareness neurons have been discovered and understood, humanity will need to reconsider its standards and return to the realization that we should as humans care for each other, that we are all members of one family and that our salvation lies in our own bewilderingly efficient brains.

I believe there is basic goodwill in mankind, but that unlike other animals, which work by instinct, human beings have freedom of choice. This implies an enormous responsibility. We are capable of behaving like animals in circumstances where self-preservation and the survival of the fittest is the top priority, but we also have the capacity to love our enemies and to try to gain peace by peaceful means. As travel and the dissemination of news become ever faster processes, world events are constantly and instantly made known to the inhabitants of planet earth. None of the outrages of the past could be kept hidden if they happened today, and so there is gradually a growing international awareness that all human beings are equally important for the well-being of the rest of us. 'No man is an island.' In harming others we harm the basis and justification of our own existence.

When groups of people become engaged in a common enterprise, then individual concern can take a second place to group concern. People will ignore their personal responsibilities and obey the leader. At the Nuremberg war-crimes trials after the Second World War, certain German commanders and officials claimed they were blameless since they were only carrying out the orders handed down to them. Nevertheless, some of those who had committed the worst betrayals of human decency were judged to be guilty and hanged. This established the important principle in international law that obeying orders should never be seen as an alibi for committing atrocities. Today we still see many frightful massacres taking place in various countries. It would become much harder for these to happen if the people concerned perceived the matter as one between individuals.

Even the most powerful democracy in the world, the United States of America, created a terrible example of this phenomenon in 1968, with the massacre at My Lai during the Vietnam war. On this occasion, Task Force Barker, a group of some 500 young American soldiers, followed their leader's orders and killed some 600 innocent villagers, old men, women and children. Apparently they had no qualms or doubts about their actions. It was war; it was their duty. It was also another terrifying illustration of how a group is capable of anything the moment it denies humanity to another group. In the case of My Lai there was no investigation until after the war had ended, and then only the task force leader was punished.

How will it ever be possible for us to lead happy and rewarding lives in the midst of so much suffering? The remedy requires constant vigilance in examining our own consciences, making sure that we do not give in to self-worship and absorption with our personal imperfections. Instead we must focus attention on the reality of what is happening around us, and be brave enough to do the best we can for the rest of humanity as we listen to the truth in our own hearts. Let us therefore make our own decisions: 'Better to light one candle than to grumble at the dark.' We have to live with ourselves. Shakespeare's Hamlet says it all:

> This above all, – to thine own self be true;
> And it must follow as night the day,
> Thou canst not then be false to any man.

I am hopeful for the future. The world is a more caring place than it was when I was a boy. I have always believed my guru in India when he said to me, 'You have nothing to fear' – an echo across many centuries of the anchoress Juliana of Norwich's great statement of spiritual optimism, 'All shall be well and all manner of things shall be well.'

I was fortunate in 1924 to have joined the Chartered Bank of India, Australia and China (today the Standard Chartered Bank); even more fortunate to have been posted to Amritsar in 1926. There I learnt Urdu, the local language, and met my guru, with whom I had many conversations about the meaning of life. Those meetings were the beginning of a whole fresh approach to the business of living and started off my interest in Buddhism. The good fortune continued when I was posted to Ceylon, Siam, French Indo-China, Malaya and China. These were all countries that had Buddhist populations and traditions and my experience of them strengthened my belief in this philosophy.

My guru in Amritsar had been a serene man with a quiet confidence and a profound interest in everything that happened about him. We were each of us, he said, a link in the chain that went back to the beginning of life on earth. While it was impossible to know the unknowable, and no one through all the generations had discovered the answer, mankind was constantly coming nearer to understanding the vast power that controls all nature.

When I commented that all leading religions claimed to worship this power, he replied that Christians, for instance, believed that their God was their Father in Heaven and claimed to be fashioned in his image, but this was a recent belief, born no more than 2,000 years ago, that had been the cause of wars and untold suffering, of tortures such as happened under the Spanish Inquisition. It was a belief that enabled men to place themselves in positions of great power and wealth, though it remained unproven that such a deity was in any way identical with the natural force that regulated everything in the universe, including the span of our lives.

Belief in religion was, of course, a deep source of comfort for those who felt certain that their God was watching over them and preparing an eternal heaven for them after they died. It also suggested that their life on earth was brief in contrast with eternity, and therefore that eternity was more important. 'Suffer crosses in this world and gain crowns in the next,' as the missionaries said.

In that case, I asked my guru, what was one to do to lead a full and enjoyable life? His reply was that it is possible to enjoy the fruits of the earth within the laws of nature, which are the same for everyone. People die because they are born. Nature provides only a limited life-span, to ensure that the new generation will not be held captive by the past.

'Seek as wide a knowledge as possible of everything,' he said. 'Respect your fellow-humans, for you exist only in their minds. Do not be lured into pursuits of power, wealth or beliefs. Nature gave us brains with which to judge ourselves. As Buddha said, "Be ye lamps unto yourselves, light your own path and be true to yourself." You have the beginnings of this in your mind. Make good use of it, then you will lead a full and possibly happy life.'

This was all very well, I responded, but did it not mean that I must become a child of nature and relinquish my religion and my nationality? If this was so, then where was I to turn for help?

All my ancestors were part of me, he replied, and each generation of them had helped me a little further along the path. Thus my support came from within. I only needed to listen quietly. Then I would hear the still small voice that was my true self.

Often we talked in this way until the sun was setting and casting long shadows across the garden. Sunset in Amritsar was always a magical moment when the scent of the orange groves emerged from the heat of the day and mingled with the smell of cooking fires. From the distance came the evening calls of peacocks. Whenever my guru rose to leave, I would ask him when I would see him again. He always gave the same reply. All the people we meet and know become a part of our lives, so we can never be parted from them. 'You have nothing to fear,' he would say again with a friendly smile.

The evening arrived when we spoke together for the last time. As he departed in the dusk, I watched his little figure walk down the drive to the earth road, where he turned and waved.

1

The Dart of Life

The astronaut William Anders said when he returned from circling the moon in Apollo 8: 'We looked back from 240,000 miles to see a very small, round, beautiful, fragile-looking little ball floating in an immense black void of space. It was the only colour in the universe – very fragile – very delicate indeed. Since it was Christmas time it reminded me of a Christmas-tree ornament – colourful and fragile. Something we needed to handle with care.'

This is the spinning ball at which nature hurls our darts of life, each of which carries the genes and instincts of our million ancestors. Where the dart strikes for us will decide our nationality, colour and religion, and possibly even our political outlook. The vast variety of potential destinies is bewildering. Who would deliberately choose to be born into an African state that was prone to civil war and famine? Wherever the dart may land, however, birth and death become inevitable.

Yet there is an advantage to be gained from facing the

fact that there is both beginning and end to personal existence: we insure our lives so that our deaths may benefit
others. Decisions become simpler, priorities sharpen their
perspective, once the realization dawns that we may not be
around tomorrow. Time is the most precious gift that life
has to offer, and none of us can know what our allocation
of it may be. The Arabian peoples believe that the fates of
men are written in the sand; the Druzes that there is a
book in which their dates of birth and death are recorded,
and that no mortal disaster can befall them until the crucial
moment arrives. The important message conveyed by time
is not to waste it: to live with the present moment, not in
the future, and certainly not in the past. Enjoy yourself
now. We are creatures of enjoyment and the capacity to
enjoy is another of the gifts of time, even if certain negative
strains of puritan thinking would have us think otherwise.
Of course, the counter-image of enjoyment is suffering,
and this we must also accept as a part of the wholeness of
experience. But meanwhile, as the old song goes, 'It is later
than you think.' The world wasn't made yesterday and the
saddest words in any language are, 'Too late.'

What, then, ought to be the starting-point? First there
are the treasures of the home country to be explored.
Parents and families should nourish the richness of intuitive
experience offered by historical sites, ancient battlefields,
old villages, churches, cathedrals, folk museums, relics of
the past. We cannot afford to allow these things to be
dealt with only under the compartmentalized heading of
'education'. Knowing and absorbing our past helps us to
understand our present and to plan our future. As we grow
older, theatres, art galleries, concert halls all offer the chance
for further enrichment. We may also learn to appreciate
good food and wine. Like the rest, it requires study, but
the time and effort involved will be repaid many times over.

The world is a many-splendoured thing. Curiosity is a
natural teacher: those who manage to stimulate it for them-

selves will never be bored, whatever their age. It is true, though, that we learn best and most effortlessly when we are young, especially when our imaginations are fired. This is why whatever happens to inspire the imaginations of young people is so important to each of them as individuals. Yet all should beware of making wealth and fame the spur. Like Kipling's 'triumph and disaster', they are two impostors. Life is for living, so why strive to be famous? Fame or wealth, if they do come to us, only define us in the most superficial sense. True values lie elsewhere. The celebrities of a season are tomorrow's forgotten people. So-called 'fame', in the hectic media interest of the modern world, has become utterly ephemeral. The famous are famous for fifteen minutes, to adapt Andy Warhol's notorious prediction.

As far as living is concerned, the human race does not, alas, learn collectively from experience. Throughout life we need to be wary of causes which claim any right to seek the control of people's hearts and minds; they end in the slaughter of the innocents. The endless cemeteries of the two world wars and the well-chronicled massacre of six million Jews provide reminders of where our tragic weaknesses lie, if any were needed. Almost every day the television news provides us with further examples. We are born savages, and while we are capable of attaining nobility, the veneer of civilization is all too fragile.

Meanwhile, aside from the wars and humanitarian disasters, the joy of living is something else, a positive counterbalancing force. Paris provides a fine example of a capacity for enjoyment in action, a lovely city overflowing with a zest to exist. Her theatres, museums, art galleries, restaurants, cafés, gardens, cathedrals, her Seine river – wherever one looks there are fresh delights awaiting discovery. Here the joy of living is never questioned. Such joy should be the beginning of everyone's world exploration, whether we are speaking of the great world outside ourselves or the inner world that we carry about inside our heads. Up until now we have discovered and classified some 1.4 million species of plants and animals out of approximately 100 million. Perhaps we should therefore be devoting a small fraction of the resources we spend on space research to exploring the still undiscovered riches of our own planet. The great treasures of the natural world remain out there, unspoilt, waiting for all who wish to enjoy them.

It is in many ways a mistake to reserve the education of travel for retirement, by which time the mind is burdened and the benefits may come too late. Therefore those who have been able to begin their travels in the fullness of youth, when the world was still packed with surprises and everything fresh, everything quickly absorbed, are fortunate. Today one of the effects of television has been to render many wonders of nature and exotic scenes over-familiar, in a superficial sense, at least. It may well therefore be harder for future generations to capture a vision of the new. Freshness has become more difficult to find; aeroplanes fly us to the most remote corners of the earth in hours rather than days. Such journeys used to take months, of course, and travel by air can never replace the feeling of adventure offered by travels by land or sea. Each airport is depressingly like every other airport, and the same applies to the international hotels that have sprung up in almost all the lovely, previously unspoilt regions of the world. Journeys by sea in particular allow time for travellers to enjoy the stimulation of encountering new people and customs – time to adapt to other ways of life, time to savour a slow progress through strange new scenes towards a distant destination. Going by air means that time is saved, but only at the cost of a loss of romance. 'Half our life is spent trying to find something to do with the time we have rushed through life trying to save,' said the American comedian Will Rogers as long ago as 1930 – an insight even more true today.

Fortunately many of the old hotels from a former, more

leisurely age have survived, including, for instance, the Cataract Hotel at Aswan, to which the original Thomas Cook dispatched his customers to spend warm and sunny winters away from a freezing Europe. Ports and railway stations still retain a sense of excitement, and ships and trains remain the cheapest form of transport. Youth in search of adventure can still, if it is determined enough, find access to the wilder side of life through enrolling with such organizations as Voluntary Service Overseas – a commitment that may also help to focus the natural idealism of the young and bring home lessons in some of the realities of life on this planet. Ease of movement around the globe today provides a vast choice of situations, with virtually every country in the world open to the dedicated job-hunter.

On the other hand, it also needs to be recognized that not everyone has the chance to travel. Ill-health or other reasons may make the prospect impracticable. Our inner journeys, however, are of equal if not of even more importance. They open the way to both self-discovery and the vast and sometimes dark continents of art, literature and music. The gifts, rewards and values of these are capable of coming alive for each of us. There is also the search for knowledge, and the opportunities offered by many small schools of arts and crafts. Here, in Britain, we are fortunate to have the Open University, which has given so many people renewed opportunities right across a range of age-groups. The quest for knowledge may well be the most broadly creative and important exploration of all, for it is one that will fill the mind and comfort its owner for life.

Since it is true that we live in other people's minds, we should let nothing – caste, colour, class, title, creed or other barrier – be a source of separation between ourselves and others. The greater the wisdom of those others, then the less likely they are to be concerned about their own social position and status, however humble or exalted it may be. Among human categories we can say that snobs and social climbers have less than most to offer. As Thomas Grey wrote in his *Elegy in a Country Churchyard*:

Can storied urn or animated bust
Back to its mansion call the fleeting breath?
Can Honour's voice provoke the silent dust,
Or Flattery sooth the dull cold ear of Death?

The lesson which travel teaches us is to be receptive, not protective. It does not matter what people think of you. There is no purpose in behaving as if you were important. 'He that is low need fear no fall.' Be like a sponge; soak up new experiences. To say a welcoming 'Yes' to experience is clearly better than avoiding it for fear of having one's battlements of self-defence breached by an imagined enemy. Your regrets when you die are likely to be not for the multitude of mistakes you made but for the things you left undone. From this it follows that it is never too early to start. There is nothing to fear but fear itself. One learns to ride by falling off horses and having the courage to remount. It is never too late in life to go on mounting our metaphorical horses. The young these days often seem to scorn humble jobs and responsibilities, but if that is so they are making a great mistake. Work will be the key to all that follows in their lives, and the craft of dealing with a set of circumstances within a group of fellow-workers should be taken seriously at every level. Many of the failures in industry have been, and continue to be, failures in management.

'Never be lulled' is the invaluable message of experience. Everything may appear to be running with perfect smoothness, but we should always allow for a 'fumble factor' of at least 10 per cent. Decent, reasonable, trustworthy people have, time and again, given their assurance that a situation will turn out all right in the end, only to find themselves being overtaken by crisis and disaster. It can be a hazardous slackness if you fail to check and double-check every situation until the reality becomes crystal-clear. Write down those things that need to be answered before going into a meeting, especially if it is with a doctor. If you suffer from shyness, make up your mind that you are going to overcome it. Getting into the way of talking to everyone you encounter, no matter who they are, is always the surest, quickest technique for finding yourself.

Among all the many ways there are of seeing the world, banking may not seem, on the face of it, to be among the most adventurous, but the seeds of modern banking were sown 60,000 years ago, when barter was the sole currency. Tribes skilled in stone cutting exchanged their stone and flint knives, arrowheads and axe-heads with other tribes who produced wooden objects, such as hafts, spear shafts and throwing sticks. Fishing tribes exchanged fish for meat and so on. Barter formed links between different tribes and bypassed nationality, politics and religion. Traders formed their own international laws. To survive they needed to be trusted and to understand fully one another's needs, but the driving force above all others was gain. The same impetus and benefits today maintain modern banking, a profession that has produced Britain's youngest prime minister this century in John Major, who joined the Standard Chartered Bank and later claimed it had been his university, as it was mine a generation or two earlier.

Working for such a bank gives a thorough grounding in the realities of international finance and provides stimulation and excitement in abundance. In a hundred countries the Standard Chartered Bank services millionaires, princes of the earth, wealthy manufacturers, small businessmen, planters of rubber, tea and coffee, dealers in hides and skins, carpets, cotton, silk, precious stones and much, much more. Trading among the entrepôts of the East is an exciting if risky game, in which the banker acts as referee. The profession offers a ringside seat for all that is going on: the daring deals, the hopes and fears, the failures and successes.

At the end of the day it is the banker to whom every protagonist turns, and it is the interests of trade rather than political manipulation that hold out the best hope of success in any of the so-called 'peace processes' between formerly hostile factions or countries.

Yet, whatever the task in life that emerges as being most suited to our personalities and abilities, we all continue to need Rudyard Kipling's trusty henchmen – 'what, why, when, how, where and whom' – to whet our curiosity. The advice of my father was sound and concise: 'Moderation in all things,' coupled with his old printer's adage, 'When in doubt leave out.' The advice of an uncle, who was a distinguished medical man and knew what he was talking about, had always been, 'Leave well alone.'

2

Faith

The last surviving wonder of the world, the Great Pyramid of Cheops, is a monument to the dawn of modern religion. The Ancient Egyptians were happy, life-loving people, who were in awe of death. Taking advantage of this fear, their kings proclaimed themselves to be Pharaohs, god-kings, and offered eternal life to those who did their will. They formed a priesthood that wore special garments, prayed, burnt incense, made libations with holy water and assured worshippers that they would, after they had died, live again in paradise for ever, provided they broke none of the divine laws decreed by the god-kings.

All the garments that have gone to clothe later religions were originally woven in Ancient Egypt. As a system of belief theirs was a formidable creed. The priests had well-feathered nests, the wealthy were given security in the here and now, and the workers believed the assurance that their labours in this world would be rewarded with security and abundance in the next, provided they obeyed the will of the Pharaohs. Today's religions would have little appeal if they did not hold out more or less the same promise.

Despite being given the protection of the largest man-made building structure in the world, the mummy of Cheops, laid to rest in 2690 BC, has vanished, stolen for its sacred jewellery and precious tablets of gold that were to see the soul of Cheops safely on its journey into the next world. Under the Pharaohs, minor gods and goddesses multiplied until every community had its own special god. Cat, crocodile, jackal, snake and vulture gods flourished and the people had faith in them to respond to their needs and guard their interests.

Yet even among the Pharaohs there was one enlightened man who proclaimed a rationalistic monotheism, based on a worship of the disc of the sun, which, he perceived, was the very source of life, light, warmth and abundance on earth. This was Akhenaten (1379–1362 BC), the husband of the legendary beauty, Queen Nefertiti, and, some think, the father of Tutankhamun. Akhenaten proclaimed the cult of Aten, the supreme being, and one of the hymns he wrote in his praise survived at El Amarna on the tomb walls. It is one of the timeless masterpieces in visionary literature:

When thou risest in the morning and shinest as Aten by day thou dost put to flight the darkness and givest forth thy rays. The Two Lands rejoice, they awake and stand on their feet, for thou hast aroused them. They wash their limbs and take up their clothes, their arms do adoration to thy rising. All the land performs its labours. All cattle rejoice in their pastures. The trees and herbs grow green. Birds and winged things come forth from their nests, their wings doing adoration to thy spirit. All goats skip on their feet, all that flies takes wing; they begin to live when thou risest on them. Ships ply upstream and downstream likewise; every path is opened by reason of thy rising. The fish in the stream leap before thy face, thy beams are in the depths of the ocean. Creator of issue in women, maker of seed in mankind, who quickenest the son in the womb of his mother, soothing him that he may not weep, nurse within the womb, who givest breath to quicken all whom he would create. When he comes forth from the womb in the day of his birth thou dost open his mouth and dost provide for his needs. When the chick in the egg cries within the shell thou givest him breath within it to quicken him; thou hast made for him his strength to break from within the egg. When he comes forth from the egg to chirp with all his might he goes upon his two legs when he comes forth from it.

How manifold are thy works! They are concealed from us. O sole god to whom no other is like! Thou didst create the earth according to thy desire when thou wast alone, men and cattle, all goats, all that is upon the earth and goeth upon its feet, and all that is in the sky and flieth with its wings. The foreign lands too, Syria and Ethiopia, and the land of Egypt. Thou puttest each man in his place, thou providest for his needs, each having his sustenance and his days reckoned. Their tongues are distinguished in speech; their characters likewise and their complexions are different. Thou has distinguished the nations.

Thou createst the Nile in the Underworld and bringest it forth according to thy will to give life to mankind, even as thou didst create them for thyself, lord of all of them, who art weary by reason of them, lord of every land, who risest for them, Disk of the day, great of might. Thou art in my heart. There is none other that knoweth thee save thy son Akhenaten. Thou didst grant him to understand thy counsels and thy might when the earth came into being in thy hand; even as thou didst make them.

When thou risest they live, when thou settest they die.
Thou art length of days in thyself. In thee men live.
Eyes are on thy beauty until thou settest. All labour is
set aside when thou settest in the west: but when thou
risest work for the king is made to proceed apace. All
men that run upon their feet since thou didst found
the earth thou has raised them up for thy son who
came forth from thyself, even Akhenaten.

(Sir Alan Gardiner, *Egypt of the Pharaohs*)

The doctrines of Akhenaten did not survive his death,
after which the priests and people returned to their old
ways and a multiplicity of deities. If only his ideas had
caught on at that stage, then we might all have been saved
a lot of trouble.

Today humankind requires something more than faith
when it comes to travelling in this world, let alone the
next. Each of the liners that carry passengers across vast
oceans is under the command of a captain who, like the
Pharaohs, has absolute authority within his own domain.
His ship is a self-contained community that has all the
advantages of a city – law and order, heating and lighting,
food – which is also in constant touch with the outside
world. It even has its own well-equipped hospital. The ship
is efficiently run by people of widely differing nationalities
and religions, serving an even wider spectrum of passengers.
When the time comes for an officer on watch to be relieved,
his relief does not merely accept a verbal account of the
situation as he takes over the duty. Before he can do so,
the course, speed and all other functions need to be checked
and double-checked against the ship's instruments, which
are the finest available. The same standard of care applies
aboard any well-run airliner.

Humankind has grown to be confident of its place in
the universe, even though the reasoning is questionable.
Life on earth depends on water in the atmosphere and

energy supplied by the sun. Had our planet been any closer to that rather small star, then the water would have remained in a constant state of vapour. Had it been any farther away, then the water would have remained frozen solid. There is no guarantee that this happily balanced condition which allows us to exist is going to last for ever. It was in the seas that life began, and when the early creatures produced by the creative forces of evolution began to crawl on to dry land, they brought the water with them, inside their skins – the first space suits. Mankind still has the sea in its blood, which still tastes of salt. But the immensity of the endless sea, the sky above it filled with stars, the boiling thrust of brilliant water, make most of us feel very small beside the vastness of the universe.

Does the enormous force that drives nature have regard for the latest and cleverest animal that happens to live on one small planet among countless millions? Is this force something that may be made use of or turned to for help? The answer to both these questions is an emphatic, 'Yes,' though it still needs to be qualified, for it is clear that this vast power does not care for weakness. The survival of the fittest is its law. On the other hand, science is learning steadily more about nature and is rapidly overcoming many problems that seemed intractable in the past. The weak can indeed be made strong; faith in science and the knowledge it brings will be the source of our salvation in the end.

The longevity and success of the British Empire could be attributed to the ability of the British – a 'mongrel' people, according to Daniel Defoe – to appreciate the needs of those who became its subjects under their administration. The British did not seek to change customs or religion within their dominions; their subjects had trust in them and their ability to administrate. The missionaries who followed close on the heels of trade as new countries and markets opened up lost no time in working hard to save 'the heathen', and many spent their entire mature lives spreading the 'Word of God', setting up schools and hospitals and tending the poor and destitute. Mother Teresa of Calcutta provides a famous latter-day example of this approach, though a point of criticism levelled against her has been that she offers love rather than skilled medical help.

One particular problem facing the missionaries was the rivalry between the competing Christian Churches, Roman Catholic, Church of England, Presbyterian, Methodist and another thirty or more smaller denominations, each claiming to have access to a correct version of the truth and denying any such status to their competitors in the field. This led to confusion among 'the heathen', who were often more logical than they were given credit for and could not understand why there should be such conflicts between Christians who all claimed to worship the same God. Despite the best efforts of the missionaries, the numbers of their converts remained few, but whatever feelings the new set of beliefs aroused, the peoples they lived among were glad to have the schools, medical services and, especially for the untouchables in India, a recognition as equals.

The people the missionaries came to save had older religions, ranging from animistic beliefs to complex, sophisticated mythologies and methods of worship. It seems odd that these were so seldom acknowledged, studied or even in part incorporated, for common ground did exist and perhaps the best of both might with profit have been blended. Buddhism and Christianity certainly share many areas of similarity in their ethical aims. The Sikh religion, to take another example, sensibly holds that God is interested not in religious labels but in the way we conduct ourselves – a lesson badly needed by Christianity. The ancestor worship in China, which started 2,000 years before Christ, has produced a more caring attitude to the elderly than it would be possible to find today in any of the present-day so-called 'Christian' societies. Nor should we ever forget that both the world wars of the twentieth century were essentially Christian wars.

In civic matters, the decisions of the British administrators were accepted in the interests of fair play, like those of cricket umpires. Indeed, cricket became the most popular sport in their dominions, and continues to be so, with ever-increasing importance, in many former colonial countries, despite the fact that the zenith of the greatest empire the world has known lies far in the past by now. Examples of this confidence in principles of British fair play sometimes occurred during the early-morning ride of a British resident, as I can vouch for from my own experience in India. A pair of Indian neighbours would stop the rider and ask him to settle a dispute between them. When they were asked why they did not take their case to court, they would reply that one of them was a Hindu and the other a Moslem, and hence, if they went to court, then the magistrate would himself be either a Hindu or a Moslem, and so unable to give them the unbiased opinion they could expect from a European.

The Indian Empire was a country of 370 million, with many seditious organizations; the British presence was tiny, consisting of 1,800 civil servants, 4,000 police and 65,000 army. India could have thrown out all the colonial personnel at any time it pleased her to do so, except that religion divided her peoples. Meanwhile, like the Pharaohs, the British possessed an unbounded faith in their own ability to govern, which helped them to maintain the bluff. It was all a matter of faith. As I had seen earlier in my life, the evangelists in Ulster had been drawn from a host of denominations, each one certain that it alone held the key to the truth and that the others were in error. The Hindus, for their part, had faith in their caste system and their innumerable gods and goddesses, locked into many complex strata of philosophical belief. The Moslems held to Allah and the Koran. Only Buddha had preached a philosophy without God or soul, and one that did not require faith, but his followers soon provided him, too, with the trappings of divinity. Christ often stated that he was the son of man, and when his disciples said he was surely the Son of God, he charged them to tell that to no man. Dogmas requiring faith have been shown to be mistaken in the past and will be proved wrong again in the future.

After the Pharaohs, many wise men, prophets and philosophers emerged from the multitudes of people on planet earth. Their visions of love and goodness and the unity of creation gained a host of followers, but were then taken over by religions, dragooned, paraded and institutionalized to serve systems of belief. Herein perhaps lay the greatest tragedy that humanity has ever suffered. As the divinity of the teachers was proclaimed, so temples were built and vast organizations arose that came under the control of hierarchies of powerful priests. The simple messages of the founders were hijacked and distorted, transformed into elaborate rituals that were designed to emphasize exclusiveness. The new orders promised eternal life to their adherents, but at a fearful cost to any who dared question their central authority. So history has come to be filled with its records of the persecution of the innocents; with the countless thousands burnt at the stake in a cruelty arising from the perverse notion that this would save their immortal souls; with the onset of the wars of religion, fought to increase the formidable power of one faith or another, each claiming to possess the secret of the only true path when the real motive was political and social control.

Amid all this clamour for 'certainty' the one thing of which we may be sure is that the power that created the universe is still awaiting discovery. Yet all religions, and all sectarian divisions within those religions, still claim for their god the distinction of being *the* creator of the universe and everything it contains. It is a point that Aldous Huxley puts into perspective in his essay, 'One and Many': 'There are many kinds of Gods. Therefore there are many kinds of men. For men make Gods in their own likeness. To talk about religion except in terms of human psychology is an irrelevance.' The consequence has been continual strife between the different faiths, while the natural laws go majestically on their way, unchanged and never changing, regardless of the petty struggles among the creatures they have brought into being. Nature is wild, beautiful and bountiful; destructive and creative; her animals, including all of us, are frequently filled with joy and laughter. It seems constantly strange that, in the whole epic expanse of the Bible, its numerous writers should have found virtually no place for humour. But then humour is subversive and paradoxical; at its most effective it stands certainties on their head.

Our present religious faiths are disruptive; the original message to love one another and to respect our neighbours is being lost and replaced by bitterness and bloodshed. As Pandit Nehru expressed it: 'Politics and religion are obsolete. The time has come for science and spirituality.' Nationality, colour and patriotism are other factors that divide humanity. Nature has given us magnificent brains, which are capable of realizing that her laws remain constant and of planning our lives in relation to those laws. The response of Buddha was to advise us to consider these matters quietly and objectively and to work out our own salvation. The universe operates with tremendous power and minute precision. Surely it is a stunning arrogance to assume or claim that this supreme force could be anything like us, or vice versa. Perhaps, however, it is a power that may be tapped for help, strength and reassurance. Many have experienced extrasensory perception, and the insight of the genuine mystics, which has given them a fleeting but profound vision of the unity of creation, has enhanced life quite independently of the barriers of religious dogma.

Few have described this with a more beautiful simplicity than William Blake:

> To see a World in a Grain of Sand
> And a Heaven in a Wild Flower,
> Hold infinity in the palm of your hand
> And eternity in an hour.

In fact we are talking about something that might be called self-help; or, as Oliver Cromwell said, 'Trust in God, but keep your powder dry.' Will Rogers had a way of striking nails on the head with a hammer of wit, and I believe it was he who said: 'Faith is believing what ye know ain't so.' Confucius, the founder of the great world religion of Confucianism in about 500 BC, was not concerned with the supernatural but made his appeal to reason instead. He taught that love and respect for one's fellows was superior to ambition, charity, forgiveness or repentance. Neither he nor Buddha taught of a life after death. There was enough to be getting on with in this world without fretting about a hereafter.

Man is the only animal to kill his own kind in large numbers, and he does it, as often as not, in the cause either of religion or, in our own century, of ideologies that turned out in practice to be pseudo-religions. The creation of the 'Thousand-Year Reich' of the German Nazi party or the 'New Jerusalem' of the dialectical materialists have both been used to justify some of the most monstrous acts carried out by *Homo sapiens* against fellow-humans. As the psychotherapist Anthony Storr has written in his study, *Human Aggression*, we can hardly dispute that man is aggressive:

> With the exception of certain rodents, no other vertebrate habitually destroys members of its own species. No other animal takes positive pleasure in the exercise of cruelty upon another of his own kind . . . The

sombre fact is that we are the cruelest and most ruthless species that has ever walked the earth . . . One difficulty is that there is no clear dividing line between those forms of aggression which we all deplore and those which we must not disown if we are to survive.

Jacob Bronowski, at a memorable point in his distinguished television series, *The Ascent of Man*, stood in the shallow water at the edge of the pond into which the human ashes from the Auschwitz crematoria had been flushed, and gathered up a handful of mud. Mingled among the ashes were those of many members of his own family. 'When people believe that they have absolute knowledge, with no test in reality, this is how they behave,' he said. 'This is what men do when they aspire to the knowledge of gods.' They have continued so behaving in many parts of the world, including, I am grieved to say, my Ulster homeland. 'You can't say civilization don't advance, however, for in every war they kill you in a new way' – Will Rogers again.

But our aggression is a two-edged sword. In the words of Dr Storr, the 'tragic paradox [is] that the very qualities which have led to man's extraordinary success are also those most likely to destroy him'. Perhaps if we could rid ourselves of notions and promises of paradise in both the next world and the present one, then it might lead to more concern for the preservation of life and being while these conditions actually last.

Arthur C. Clarke, famous for his uncanny insights into the future, certainly gives expression to the more optimistic long-term view when he writes in *Profiles of the Future*:

Our galaxy is now in the brief springtime of its life – a springtime made glorious by such brilliant blue-white stars as Vega and Sirius, and, on a more humble scale, our own sun. Not until these have flamed through their incandescent youth, in a few fleeting billions of years, will the real history of the universe begin.

It will be a history only illuminated by the reds and infra-reds of dully-glowing stars that would be almost invisible to our eyes; yet the sombre hues of that all-but-eternal universe may be full of colour and beauty to whatever strange beings have adapted to it. They will know that before them lie, not the millions of years in which we measure eras of geology, nor the billions of years which span the past lives of the stars, but years to be counted literally in trillions.

They will have time enough, in these endless aeons, to attempt all things, and to gather all knowledge. They will not be like gods, because no gods imagined by our minds have ever possessed the powers they will command. But for all that, they may envy us, basking in the bright afterglow of Creation; for we knew the Universe when it was young.

3

The Senses

In my youth I was taught that my brain controlled bodily functions, that my heart controlled feelings of love and hate, and that, most importantly, I possessed an immortal soul, and this belonged to God. Upon the resurrection of my body, as the Last Trump sounded, I would be restored to life, to dwell for ever in heaven, or, if I failed to qualify, to suffer in hell for eternity. It was also said by many that they felt the truth of a thing, such as their beliefs, in their livers, bones, bowels, blood and water.

As we have seen, the unknown force that set the universe in motion and holds it on course is itself for many the god of their religion. My own belief is that some people are able to tap into this force, that somewhere in our unconscious we have links that provide points of contact with this ultimate source of inanimate and conscious being. Psychology and psychiatry have, from below the surface of our personalities, peeled away the layers out of which our impulses spring. The confessional of the Roman Catholic

Church and the meditation of Zen both work in their own spheres, but where religions separate people, science and knowledge thankfully unite them.

Science continues to uncover nature's secrets and can predict with accuracy certain future events and cure diseases previously untreatable. Within one generation we have seen astonishing progress. Outer space has been explored, men have walked on the moon and, for the first time in the long history of astronomy, seen its far side. Science should now be acceptable to all religions. We need to wipe our mental slates clean and let them be reinscribed in the clear light of reality, though debates on all the implications will undoubtedly continue. As was reported in the *Financial Times* for 23/24 January 1993:

> Stephen Hawking, one of the experts invited to read papers and debate with Papal theologians, was invited to an audience with the Pope. The Pope told him that it was all right to study the evolution of the Universe after the Big Bang, but we should not inquire into the Big Bang itself because that was the moment of creation and the work of God. Hawking had argued that space-time was possibly infinite, with no boundary, and therefore there could be no moment of creation.

Some people have a sixth sense, which sometimes predicts impending danger. It may be similar to the electric preceptors possessed by sharks, which can detect one 200 millionths of a volt and thus allow them to obtain a fix on the positions of prey or enemies over great distances. Everyone has, at some time or another, experienced an instinctive dislike for a total stranger, or a sense of threat or danger that we cannot articulate or explain in a rational way:

I do not like thee, Dr Fell,
The reason why I cannot tell,
But this I know and know full well,
I do not like thee, Dr Fell.

We need to become attuned to our instincts, so that we can recognize when we reach a point when we should decide to hold our peace and say nothing – to pay attention to a flash of perception. It may be that these matters have to do with self-preservation in a hostile environment. An instinctive liking for a stranger may also, similarly, have to do with survival. It is an advantage to be among our own kind, so long as the circle never closes into a clique. The confidence-trickster inspires a special outrage: he has learnt the knack of allaying our natural suspicions while exploiting our wish to trust. In the area of relationships, the word 'chemistry' has come to have an extensive use in attempts to account for our human patterns of mutual attraction and rejection. We say we 'fall in' love, and perhaps even that may have something to do with our bodies' electrical circuits.

Everything in the world is, when reduced to its smallest component, made up of the same fundamental particles. We may not understand the nature of these completely, but the quarks and other particles are the building bricks of the universe and everything that exists, from atoms to the human race. The never-ending cycles of formation and decay of these particles represent the timeless 'dance of life' of the universe. Out of these components our senses conjure up for us the seemingly solid world in which we live.

The real world is a whirling mass of electrical charges that are virtually immortal, though the concept of this is hard for us to accept or comprehend. The still and silent times and spaces so dear to us are only still and silent because of the limitations of our senses. In reality they are filled with a turmoil of sound and images that we cannot hear or see. Television and radio receivers have abilities of perception that we lack.

The whirling masses of electric particles, consisting of nothing but energy, are not apparent to our senses until they go through processes of combining into various formations, beginning with atoms. The atoms then combine, in turn, to make molecules, a molecule being the smallest piece of matter to which a substance can be reduced without it losing its nature. Molecules, like their components, are full of movement. A drop of colour in a filled bath will quickly spread throughout the water. If a glass of water is poured into the sea, then this same constant movement will in time disperse the molecules the glass contained throughout all the oceans of the world. Eventually a random glassful taken from any part of the oceans will contain at least one of those original molecules. It is because of this rapid dispersal of liquid molecules that even small amounts of liquid insecticide are capable of contaminating huge quantities of drinking water. They persist in the oceans – and hence in the food chains of sea animals and birds and ultimately ourselves. Molecules are no respecters of persons. Some of those you drink in your glass of wine today have already passed through the bladders of Julius Caesar, Pontius Pilate and Queen Victoria, not to mention the entire animal kingdom.

All knowledge, and all appreciation of knowledge, is located in one highly complex organ, the brain. On my eighty-eighth birthday I had a cataract removed from my right eye and replaced with a lens. The surgeon used a local anaesthetic, which meant I remained wholly conscious and, during the operation, saw sights I had never dreamed of: a dazzling, scintillating display of coloured lights, forming and reforming like a galaxy of wonderful fireworks. My eye went on to demonstrate its capabilities superbly. Immediately after the operation I found that the world had ceased to be dark and hazy, but had instead become clear and bright – very bright. I asked to examine the old lens. It was yellow and opaque, and it was impossible to see through it. It was identical with the cataract that was still in my left eye, yet now, if I covered my right eye, I could manage to see through the opaque lens in the left eye. Somehow my brain was able to compensate for the handicap of the remaining cataract.

Even more astonishing was the effect I found when I covered my left eye and looked exclusively through my new lens. Although everything became bright and exquisitely sharp in focus, there was no sense of depth, for it requires two eyes to give perspective. But the most remarkable discovery was still to come. When I opened both eyes I found that, although the brightness of the scene was undiminished, the bad eye gave the correct perspective. My brain, in other words, was able to obtain the very best result from the circumstances with which it found itself dealing.

During millions of generations the brain seems, in effect, to have evolved into a vast reservoir of experience accumulated and passed down from one generation to the next. The possession of this experience seems, in turn, to have given it the 'sixth sense' which transmits warnings of danger. Without it and its attributes, we could not hope to survive our journey through life or call on it to bring common sense to our decision-making. It remains light-years ahead of the most sophisticated computers.

How, then, does the brain – a soft lump of grey matter weighing slightly over three pounds and composed largely of water – perform its formidable tasks? It contains 14,000 million nerve cells, joined and cross-referenced by an astounding million billion connections to enable it to file and recall everything that happens during our lifetime, besides storing information from the past. It controls all bodily functions, understands and evaluates information received by our five senses and provides for all our conscious living. Like our bodies, the more it is exercised, the stronger it grows and the more effectively it operates.

The brain is a delicate organ, almost like a jelly in texture. It is physically guarded by the bone of our skulls, though this does not protect it sufficiently to prevent it suffering damage from the sort of heavy blows to the head received in boxing, which set it bouncing against the walls of its confined space. Alcohol in excess and certain drugs also damage the brain and disturb its function, and therefore distort perceptions of reality. The drug called 'crack', based on refined cocaine, has led to violence and murder in the United States, and it has found its way to Britain, where it has been one cause of increasing crimes of violence. The intense 'high' it provides lasts only a few seconds, but it is one of the most addictive drugs known and makes many of its users highly aggressive, bringing them to a point where nothing matters to them beyond obtaining the means to buy the next 'fix'.

In the international perspective, drug abuse may prove to be an even more deadly foe than war. It now often starts with the very young, when toxic assaults on the central nervous system are likely to have the least repairable effects, psychologically as well as chemically. Too little is known about why some young people are more vulnerable to drug habits than others, in the same way that we still know very little about why certain personalities are more liable than others to become alcoholics. Social and psychological conditions, metabolic and genetic predispositions, the pressures on the young from their own peer groups, are all factors that come into the picture. The fact is that the cornucopia of drugs at present available is a source of emotional crippling and destruction for many young people, and that in the battle of the authorities against the drugs barons and dealers it seems to be the latter group who are in the winning position.

All the way from the international smuggling operations

of the mafias to the neighbourhood street-corner world of the petty dealers, a fatal combination of money and power provides and drives the motivation. There have been many examples of unholy alliances between the drugs barons and the warlords of the modern world, and other murderous groups, who are ruthlessly willing to use drugs money to pay for and build their stockpiles of weaponry. At the end of the day it is only possible to ask whatever value there can be in accumulating such enormous illicit wealth and power, and what happiness or satisfaction could exist for a life lived among gangland rivals who are ever ready to betray or kill, quite apart from the tragedies of those who die in the factional or sectarian wars, caught in the cross-fire.

Since most official attempts to curb the flow of drugs end in outflanking and defeat, the best hope for the future seems to be a new generation of young people who will, out of idealism, react against the spurious claims that have been made for drugs, often by those who should have known better. This will need to be their decision, taken in the light of a perception of how even an occasional trans-action with their friendly neighbourhood drugs dealer is both contributing to the ugliness of the world that the drugs scene creates and sharing in the responsibility for those who suffer or die because of it.

Psychological damage to the brain can be as drastic and long-lasting as physical damage, and early influence can form a child's outlook for the whole of its life. The Jesuits were famously said to regard the first six years of a child's life as sufficient time in which to create a permanent mould. Reception during those years of development is at its high-est pitch, reasoning at its lowest. Some governments make use of this fact to create slaves for their regimes. Fundamen-talists of all persuasions are past masters at reducing liberal democracies to rigid dictatorships.

The effects of brain-washing do not always need to be

done by catching recruits when young, but can be achieved by offering the security of a well-defined group, something to belong to, something which purports to offer the answers for all the problems of life. Again, the hunger for 'certainty' may seduce the spirit into the false security of a set mind. The crunch comes when someone so enmeshed in a closed, exclusive sect has second thoughts; and then may not find it so easy to make their escape. In extreme cases, disagreeing with fundamental beliefs can even result in a death sentence where the person who asserts a free conscience is declared a non-person, a traitor to the group.

Where a group has a 'charismatic' leader who can spread the contagion of his own disturbed personality, then we may even find that his disciples will follow him into self-destruction, as happened with the 900 followers of the Rev. Jones, who all at his behest drank cyanide; or many of those who perished in the flames with David Koresh at Waco. Group paranoia may in fact help to create a kind of mini-state within which the outside world is perceived as an enemy and a fair target. It happened in Eugene, Oregon, where followers of the Bhagwan Shree Rajneesh not only spread salmonella bacteria in restaurants but also plotted the assassination of local officials who were attempting to curb their activities. Even more alarmingly, a similar mind set was evidently behind the more recent nerve-gas attacks on the Tokyo underground. It is notable that level of intelligence alone does not necessarily seem to be enough to render the individual personality immune to the influence of sects.

Once brain-washing has occurred, whether it has come about through custom, religion, politics or education, then it will be extremely hard for the individual to return to first principles, to re-examine the inculcated beliefs rationally. The joy of living may thus be lost, trapped in the fate of an upbringing or a conditioning. Time and again we have seen humanity divided by conflicting beliefs and the banquet of life turned into a battlefield. In all of this our brains are our hope of salvation, for they alone can stimulate the ability to reason, to examine by questioning all 'received truths' (religious and political) and guide us towards reality and choices made out of freedom rather than fear. It is necessary, above all, to be flexible in responses to new ideas and ever-eager to learn at every stage of our lives.

Since brains, like the rest of the body, need constant exercise to maintain them in good condition, they become lazy and the mechanism begins to creak if they are not kept busy. One of the commonest complaints as the years go by is loss of memory. The information is there in the brain; it simply refuses to be retrieved. Or else, by the time it resurfaces, it is irritatingly too late to be of any use. Nevertheless *it was* there in the brain, carefully filed, and *it did* emerge in the end. The important thing is not to allow blips of this kind to worry us, but to adopt strategies for getting round them. Whenever I have to introduce someone to someone else, and find the name has momentarily vanished, I always vaguely murmur something like, 'I'm sure you two have a lot in common.' This is why it is a good idea to write your postcards on the first day of a holiday, before a week of relaxation has made the prospect seem a daunting task. For the same reason, no one should retire from an active life without first providing themselves with a good supply of brain fodder.

So how should one set about exercising the brain? Crossword puzzles may sharpen our wits, but they will not challenge our opinions. Talking to people is my favourite method, though it is wise to avoid 'yes men' and advisable to seek out those with more original views, whose thoughts do not run all the time along predetermined tramlines and who do not believe that everything they read in the papers must be true. Your own views may be different from theirs: nevertheless debate it and listen to the opposition. A brief conversation can throw a fresh light on a long-held conviction. If we hold opinions, we should also be prepared to have them challenged, or even to challenge them ourselves. Maybe they will stand up to the evidence; maybe they won't. By the simple act of accepting the challenge we move a tiny fraction towards saving ourselves from becoming locked into a rigidly unchanging universe of our own creation.

In my youth, various passive pastimes were in great demand. People played patience, snakes and ladders, whist – anything to kill time. Time, the most precious gift of nature, was thereby lost. To kill time in order to stave off boredom is a negative incentive. Today there are many such ways of killing time. People become the 'couch potatoes' of the television culture; they surrender to an addiction to the tabloids, to arcade games (now holding out the promise of computer-created 'alternative universes' through 'virtual reality' techniques), to the euphoria and violence of crowds at what have come to be misleadingly called 'sporting' events. When the emphasis is on nothing but winning, it is natural that a game should turn into a punch-up, and that athletes should feel so pressurized that they are tempted to resort to cheating by using the synthetic methods of developing their bodies which are on offer from steroid drugs.

It is better to read a newspaper which provokes thinking rather than one that merely reinforces prejudices. Some in the older generation wrongly saw reading as a way of idling away time. Reading is a positive act: the reader needs to use his or her mind to sift and recreate, since words constantly reinforce knowledge and understanding. This is why literacy is both so powerful and inconvenient to governments, and why tyrants have feared it. They would much rather that their subjects were fed a diet of diverting television images than that they should think for themselves. Counter this tendency by increasing your interest in everything about you; stimulate an abundance of curiosity. How often do we

ask a question, only to be told: 'That's not my department.'
I once asked an elevator attendant in New York to let me
off at my publisher's floor, and gave him the name of the
company. 'You tell me which floor you want,' he replied.
'I'm here to run the elevator.' Another day I said to a
newsstand boy, 'I want to go to East 22nd Street.' He
grinned and replied, 'Why the hell doncha?' Smart talk. But
in New York today newspapers are bought from vending
machines and the elevators are all automated.

I was lucky as a child of five to have been given a picture
book called *Eyes and No Eyes*, which encouraged me to
look more carefully at the world in which I found myself.
I discovered, for instance, a toad in the garden which blended into its background so perfectly that I had to look very
carefully to discover it. Birds' nests were always present, but
again they were beautifully hidden. Watching the eggs
arrive and the chicks hatch was a wonderful experience,
and in this way I became more and more fascinated with
the world about me. I was seeing so many things that I had
never previously noticed. My brain, of course, had observed
everything before, but had remained uninvolved since there
was at that stage no awakening of interest. The gift of a
camera also made me aware of the multitude of things that
were happening all around me. It soon became a part of
my nature to spot incongruities in a situation and to wonder
why they should be there.

This was a habit of mind that paid a dividend many years
later. When I was producing *A Night to Remember*, the film
about the sinking of the *Titanic*, I arrived on location to
find production in progress at a point where the script
called for the passengers to be seen leaping eighty feet into
the water from the decks of the doomed liner. The stunt-
men were already dressed in genuine period cork life-
jackets, which encased their bodies from groin to chin, and
were lined up ready to jump. Had they gone ahead, the
heavy cork jackets would have caught each one of them

under the chin with a force sufficient to break the neck. My timely arrival prevented the killing or maiming of the British film industry's main stock of stunt-men. Kapok replaced the cork and the scene was filmed in safety.

The brain may benefit from a good education, but only if the interest of the scholar has been fired. Many world leaders have had little schooling, but the most successful among them always had enormous curiosity and an ability and flexibility which enabled them quickly to grasp the essentials of differing situations. Wisdom is superior to cleverness. As a story from India tells, there was once an old man who sat down under a tree in the forest. He had not been sitting there long before he saw a group of three eminent professors stop near by to examine a pile of bleached bones. 'By my knowledge,' one of them declared, 'I will cause these bones to become a skeleton' – and the bones joined together and there stood the skeleton of an animal. 'By my knowledge,' said the second professor, 'I will put flesh on this skeleton' – and there stood a Bengal tiger. 'By my knowledge,' said the third, 'I will now breathe life into this magnificent animal.' But at this point the old man stood up hastily and said, 'Worthy sirs, please pause a moment while I climb this tree.' From his vantage point he was then able to watch as the tiger began to breathe deeply and promptly ate the professors.

Not all tigers have fared so well. The sabre-toothed tiger no longer exists. It was a selective feeder, and when the animals it preferred were all eaten, it followed them into extinction. Animals which enjoy a wider choice of food tend to have better chances of survival. The same thing happens in industry. The Japanese succeeded after the Second World War because their work force was unrestricted. Many other countries were held back because lines of demarcation slowed production.

At a certain stage, beyond the teaching of knowledge, it is patient curiosity that takes the lead in the way forward.

But curiosity, the greatest teaching aid of them all, can all too easily be destroyed by parents and teachers who see only their side of the matter and have themselves settled into the tramlines. Imagination is essential to creative thinking; creative thinking is essential to the progress of art, science, technology and philosophical attitudes. Despite the limitations of teachers and teaching methods, however, there are still many gifted children who come among us to amaze the world, whose knowledge seems to spring from somewhere out of time – from that accumulation of knowledge in the profound evolutionary layers of our minds.

Jesus left home to teach at the age of twelve; Mozart wrote and played sublime music while he was still a child. A shining modern example of one who grew to fulfilment outside the bounds of conventional ideas of education is Lord Menuhin. He had no proper schooling as his childhood was given up to playing his violin to adoring audiences in the world's concert halls. As he recounts in his autobiography: 'I had no academic training at all. Only my own reading, philosophy, thought and a certain breadth of experience. In a way, my formal lack of education means that I distance myself from details and take a broader view of problems that face us.'

The basis of so much of our wisdom, art and culture was laid down centuries ago by people who had no education as we understand the term. To realize this is to realize our roots and the reason why any waste of life and its gifts is a loss to our species as a whole.

4

Body and Mind

The father of medicine is generally accepted to have been Hippocrates, a Greek born on the island of Cos in about 370 BC. In fact the Ancient Egyptians had a well-organized medical system as early as the Old Kingdom (2613–2181 BC). There were three branches of medical science: surgery, practical medicine and spiritual healing. The surgeons were known as the 'priests of the Goddess Sekhmet', the physicians represented the empirical side of medical practice and the healers used magical powers, possibly hypnosis, to bring about cures. All three groups were controlled by the inspectors of doctors, who were in turn governed by the supreme overseer of medicine for Upper and Lower Egypt.

The records show that Iry, chief of the court physicians during the Fourth Dynasty (2613–2498 BC), held the titles of 'doctor of the abdomen', 'eye doctor of the palace' and 'guardian of the royal bowel movement'. The House of Life was the medical teaching centre of the major temples. Here the doctors were taught various branches of medicine and learnt the uses of herbal remedies. Under the Ptolemies, surgeons improved their knowledge of anatomy by dissecting living criminals who were due to be executed. One can only wonder whether execution was still necessary in the wake of such scientific explorations!

Over the centuries, medical knowledge increased, but in 1905, the year in which I was born, doctors still relied on their five senses to observe and diagnose illness. X-rays were not as yet available for diagnosis. The medical profession's main armoury against illness and mishap consisted of splints, bandages and, apart from the recently introduced and versatile aspirin, a traditional hit-or-miss pharmaceutical array. The doctors of the time also had a strong measure of shrewd common sense and built their practices on word of mouth. Their most important tasks were to bring their patients into this world and see them out when the time came. They combined a genuine wizardry with a touch of charlatanism, and were trusted and respected within their communities. Those patients who had the means paid for treatment; those who lacked them were treated free. Babies were born at home; minor operations were carried out on kitchen tables vigorously scrubbed with carbolic soap. Hospitals were dreaded, and closely associated by the poor with workhouses. Even in the best hospital, an abdominal operation could carry a mortality risk of about 40 per cent.

The bond between patients and doctors was strong, however. A doctor spoke from a level of experience and learning that few of his patients could match and which gave his pronouncements an impressive authority. His presence alone was often enough to make a patient feel better. The doctor of today finds himself, by comparison, in an invidious situation. The irony of it is that he has lost the old authority at the same time as medical research has been making the most extraordinary and genuine advances in history. Side by side with this has gone the demands of patients that he should provide them with absolute solutions or miracles for all their ills, and ultimately that he should protect them from mortality. To a certain extent the medical profession has only itself to blame for this situation. Carried away by the technological wonders of the age, it seems to have come to see death as representing nothing but a defeat. A whole generation of doctors and nurses thus finds it hard to cope with the facts of death and needs training to do so humanely – a quality that often came naturally to the older generation of family physicians, who, with their bluff down-to-earth realism, 'buried their mistakes'. In this area the hospice movement has provided a much-needed counter-balancing trend in assisting the terminally ill and their rela-tives to see death as a completion and a fulfilment of the value of relationships and experience.

Meanwhile doctors have also come to be separated from their patients by a formidable array of new hi-tech instru-ments, and are, in the United Kingdom at least, servants of the state, which provides their salaries. Whenever an older GP dies or retires, the lament often goes round among his patients, 'We shan't see his like again.' Unfortunately there is little time left over for true family doctoring as it was once understood. Doctors today tend to be under siege, on the one hand from bureaucratic demands and on the other from an awareness that patients, who often show them scant respect, are liable to sue them if they feel let down. As a result of the pressures created by a combination of burgeon-ing paperwork and patient expectations, the medical pro-fession itself suffers from symptoms of stress at the present time. Thankfully from the patient's point of view, however, there continue to be many good doctors within its ranks, and time spent on finding the best possible medical atten-tion for yourself and your family is never wasted.

Doctors and specialists are as variable in quality as any other professionals, but finding the right one for you or your situation can be a matter of life or death. The same imperative applies when it comes to reassuring yourself that you will receive treatment in the best and best-administered medical institution possible. In none of this is there room for complacency. On 27 July 1993, *The Times* reported that the Royal College of Surgeons had recorded that death from hernia repair was fourteen times higher in certain parts of England than it was in others – a result of surgeons using outdated techniques. In this case the health authorities were working to correct the discrepancy, but it illustrates the point that patients need to examine the various procedures for themselves and to choose the best. We have recently seen some extreme cases of faulty procedures producing serious consequences. *The Times* for 3 October 1993, for instance, reported the example of the North Staffordshire Infirmary, where, over the course of ten years, more than a thousand patients received incorrect dosages of radiation because of a computer error.

Your questions should always be answered to your satisfaction; your relationship with your doctor should always be mutually satisfactory. Seek the opinions of trusted friends whenever you are making a decision on whom you should approach. Never be afraid to ask about any treatment being offered or to enter into any discussion it may require. If one surgeon or doctor fails to satisfy you, or gives an impression of falling short in terms of the qualities of sympathy or rapport, then seek another. You are perfectly within your rights to do so.

Biological and medical research has recently brought us to the verge of a new revolutionary field: genetic therapy and engineering, backed by the Genome project, which will, when it is complete, produce a comprehensive map of the genes carried by our DNA. Every gene that the human chromosomes contain will then be mapped and identified. Scientists have as yet barely begun to explore the far-reaching potential benefits of this immense and innovative project, but genetic engineering is already helping to remove harmful genes and establish healthier, better-adapted people and animals. This is a similar, but faster, process to nature's own genetic programme of the survival of the fittest.

In certain quarters this scientific breakthrough is feared as an unwarranted interference with nature which could take us forward into uncharted territories and open yet another Pandora's box. But those who have doubts about such 'tampering' with nature should remember that all dogs were once wolves, and that man, by intelligent selective breeding, has produced a thousand different useful varieties – herding dogs, hunting dogs, guard dogs, dogs to guide the blind, house pets among many others.

Likewise, as every beekeeper knows, success in gaining a good crop of honey from a happy hive depends on having a well-bred queen. It is only necessary to replace a bad queen with a good queen to change the entire tenor of life within a hive, since it is the queen's genes that reign throughout the hive: the 50,000 workers, the 4,000 drones and future queens. A hostile hive is difficult or even impossible to manage, as the strain of so-called 'killer bees' in Mexico has illustrated dramatically. For millennia beekeepers have therefore been utilizing genetic advantage in their own and the bees' interests.

To come forward in history and natural history to an example of the present day, many weaned babies in the United States are fed on soya milk because it has been found that cows' milk lacks some of the qualities of conferring immunity to infection that are present in the milk of human mothers. As part of a current research programme, Herman, a bull grown from a fertilized egg into which the human gene, lactoferrin, has been added, is siring calves that will, if all goes well, inherit the gene and grow into cows producing milk of better quality; and this will in turn, as a result of the lactoferrin, help those human babies fed on it to ward off infections.

Because of the onset of Aids in human populations,

blood from millions of donors now needs to be screened for the HIV virus. But here there is the prospect that, by introducing the relevant gene into pigs, these animals may be able to supply unlimited blood for mankind – blood free from any infections. Pigs are valuable animals to us and have been supplying diabetics with insulin for sixty years. The future also holds out the chance of their being bred genetically to provide a number of important organs for transplant surgery. This would help to overcome the present situation of shortage, where patients needing a transplant must await a tragedy involving the death of someone of compatible type if they are to survive themselves.

There is one thing we need to be clear about, and this is that there is no way in which man can turn back the scientific clock. For better or worse it will continue to tick on. The essential long-term view is to make the best use of science to produce, in great abundance, everything necessary for pleasant living, so that no one is left out and all are provided for. Our objective should therefore be to transform the engines of destruction into engines of construction. Let us respect and, if possible, love our neighbours on this planet – their customs and cultures – and ensure that the instinct for personal survival works for the survival of all humanity. There is a long haul ahead of us. 'The mills of God grind slowly, but they grind exceeding small.'

There is so much that can be done today to help the disabled, in small ways and large. An example which has particularly caught the public imagination is provided by Professor Stephen Hawking, who, because of an acute degenerative condition, can only speak by using an electronic machine that produces words created by the residual mobility he has in two fingers of his right hand. His lectures have been some of the best-attended in the University of Cambridge and his book, *A Brief History of Time*, remained at the top of the hardback best-seller list for over three years.

Fortunately for the medical profession, the human body is infinitely adaptable to an amazing range of misfortunes and illnesses. Every day people survive the most terrible injuries. The body also has a prodigious athletic potential, and not a year goes past without previous athletic records being broken. The winners reap rich rewards and international fame. In these heady circumstances, it is the body which gets the most praise, yet it is really the mind that creates the champion.

Our bodies are not 'us'. Much rather are they the willing horses we ride. We do not 'have' the toothache. The tooth has the ache, quite properly, in order to get us to do something about it. I was fortunate, during the six years I spent working in India in my twenties, to find the time to sit at the feet of my guru, discussing the wisdom of the ancient Hindus and the philosophy of Buddha. In this way I came to realize how, in matters of health and other situations, the mind is more important than the body. Buddha taught that the ego, which says 'I am', does not exist, but is a collection of five *skandhas* or heaps of feelings: perceptions, impulses, emotions, the body and acts of consciousness. These emotions and sensations, ideas and wishes, thoughts and memories are the components that come together to produce a person's character or personality.

This character therefore changes moment by moment, for the self is not an eternal, unchanging entity, living in everlasting immutability somewhere within us. Rather is it a bundle of constantly changing prejudices that define our personality. Like a candle-flame that appears to be constant, the self is in a state of continual change. The cells of our bodies are likewise in a state of constant change; nothing is permanent. The body is a projection of the mind, and if properly handled can achieve success in many different pursuits. The natural aggression with which everyone is born to succeed in the battle for existence is no longer the best way to survive. Understanding and sympathy will in the end win the greatest rewards. 'Blessed are the meek, for they shall inherit the earth.'

Buddha said that once self is understood and removed from the centre of one's life, and consideration for others put in its place, then living becomes less stressful, and even the prospect of death loses much of its terror. In such Buddhist countries as Thailand and Bali, the people enjoy life, smile frequently, are kind to strangers, and even conduct jolly funerals. Fear is the worst element in any disease, and here, too, the Buddhist philosophy is reassuring. Buddha did not ask people to believe in his teaching. He advised his followers to try his philosophy and reject whatever did not suit them. In short, it all became a matter of common sense, of 'suck it and see'. 'Everyone I meet is my superior in some way in that I learn from him,' said Emerson.

Our richest gift at birth is insatiable curiosity, no doubt inherited from our simian ancestors. Stimulate the natural curiosity in children and, once it is aroused, they will educate themselves. Life is for wonder and enjoyment, so let us live in the present and love humanity with toleration. Everyone is doing what they consider to be best for themselves. Try to find enjoyable work to do. 'Choose a job you love and you will never have to work a day in your life,' advised Confucius. 'The secret of success is keeping your vocation your vacation,' said Mark Twain.

Avoid entanglements, such as long-term contracts; these always involve politics and the massaging of egos. Farmers and teachers, who, like doctors, were formerly known for living to ripe old ages, now similarly carry some of the highest suicide risks, a factor in this being the unending controls levelled against them by agricultural policies and administrative burdens. But whatever our profession may be, the important thing is to remain flexible all through life

– open to new ideas and capable of transferring our learnt skills to fresh and sometimes quite unexpected tasks.

No one will ever regret doing their own thing, however humble, and self-reliancy is one of the greatest antidotes to threats of redundancy or retirement. Many have found (sometimes to their surprise) that letting go of conventional 'certainties' has had the effect of releasing them from chains of habit and false 'security'. 'Why not go out on a limb, that's where the fruit is,' said Will Rogers. Writers, painters, sculptors, musicians and people who paddle their own canoes often lead longer and more enjoyable lives, despite the fact that they have opted for lifestyles that have little about them of 'secure predictability'. The really important thing for them is that they do not have to 'play games' relating to status and pecking orders.

It is the 'I' that remains the big hurdle for Westerners in Eastern philosophies. When my son said to me, 'I cannot ride the bicycle you gave me,' I told him that this 'I' did not really exist. A week later, when he was riding the bicycle without a thought as to how he did it, I asked him what had become of the 'I' that couldn't ride the bicycle. He laughed happily and said, 'It's gone!'

My guru in India encouraged me to consider the body as a projection of the mind. 'There is nothing to fear,' as he said so frequently. When my Indian Medical Service doctor told me I was dying from malignant malaria, I asked him if I might travel from the furnace heat of Amritsar to the cool hill station of Murree. He willingly agreed, pleased and relieved not to have me pegging out on his hands. Once I was there in the hills, I found I could see things more clearly through my delirium and was able to rally my defences. The disease was a battle that raged between my bodily defenders and the invading hordes of malarial parasites. It was not the 'I' that had the disease, it was my body; and I was able to encourage my troops to overcome the enemy from the secure fortress headquarters of my mind.

My father, one of the old school, always said to his doctor when he needed to consult him, 'Please don't tell me what is wrong, just make me well.' During my years in China, I discovered that certain Chinese paid their doctors to keep them well, while payment ceased if they were ill. The Chinese Ministry of Welfare today holds people personally responsible for their own health, and anyone feeling ill must report the fact to his or her employer or face punishment.

The body consists of what it eats, and so long as its diet is varied it will receive all the nourishment it needs. Too much food will make it fat; too little will make it thin. It is as simple as that. The stomach is a docile organ that responds rapidly to habit. If you feed it three large meals a day, it will, if they do not arrive on time, rebel strongly and protest. On the other hand, hunger-strikers lose their appetites after only a few days of fasting. Every poor meal eaten is a lost opportunity. Eat frugally, but eat well. This does not mean expensive food, but it does mean good food: the distinction is there to be discovered. There is a snob attitude about food. If caviar were as plentiful as potatoes, few would bother with it. The cheap and humble baked bean is a great nutritional stand-by, unlike the proverbial sliced white loaf, made from over-refined flour, which is hardly worth anyone's time or money.

Being overweight is recognized by insurance companies as a cause of shorter lives – literally the digging of one's grave with one's own teeth! The ancient Romans also understood this, though they did not deny themselves the pleasures of the banquet and merely retired to the vomatorium with a peacock's feather. When I was forty, I found I weighed fourteen stone. I said to myself, 'When you were twenty you weighed eleven stone, and were much livelier than you are now.' Gradually I let go of the three extra stone I had been carrying everywhere and came to feel much better and fitter. I taught my stomach to live on a mug of milky coffee without sugar at 7 a.m.; a bowl of bran and cereal with honey and yoghourt at noon; and at 8 p.m. a good dinner with the best part of a bottle of wine. For fifty years my stomach has never cried out for more.

Keeping fit is a rewarding occupation. The body requires suitable exercise, regularity being more important than intense levels of activity. Choose activities that can be continued into old age. Boxing, weight-lifting, squash and team games all have to come to an end, and may all leave legacies of problems once they have to be discontinued. Old strains and injuries may return to haunt us. Highly developed muscles may turn to fat and exert a strain on the heart. The heart weighs about 340 grams and beats about seventy times a minute, pumping blood through 95,000 kilometres of tubing continually. Every pound of excess fat means that the heart has to push blood through an extra 320 kilometres of tubes.

Ambition and competitiveness are rife enough in modern life. What is the good of allowing them to carry the process of burning out, which they so easily become, into our leisure hours? Beware, too, of jogging; it has come to be regarded as a dangerous activity, especially when carried out on hard urban pavements, and is suspected of causing bone and spinal damage, even of setting off brain tumours. Swimming is probably one of the best, safest and most therapeutic of exercises; and why not? After all, it was from the sea that we came in the first place. I still begin each day with a session in the swimming pool of the apartment block where I live.

The message is to treat our bodies with as much awe, care and respect as we would any other possession, even though such advice might seem to be belied by the famous ragtime dancer and pianist, Eubie Blake, who said when he reached his hundredth birthday, 'If I'd known I was gonna live this long I'd have taken better care of myself!'

There have been four recent advances in dealing with the body and mind that encourage me to be optimistic about our future. First comes the prediction that we will soon each carry a computerized card containing our complete medical record, which will enable doctors, wherever we may be in the world, to diagnose and deal accurately with our medical problems as they arise.

Secondly, there is the prospect that human embryos will be screened for defective genes shortly after conception, and that, as techniques in gene replacement therapy advance from the theoretical to the practical area, these inimitable or damaged genes may be countermanded. Genetic predispositions are suspected in various illnesses, including some cancers, and it may prove possible to neutralize their influence. We should also be able to look forward to a time when many distressing and troublesome inherited conditions, such as muscular dystrophy, neurofibromatosis or haemophilia, become susceptible to therapy. Even the terrible familial genetic scourge of Huntington's chorea, which in middle age invariably condemns those who inherit it to an irreversible degeneration of the central nervous system, may become in due course a curiosity known only in the pages of historical medical text-books.

Thirdly, we can already see many ways in which massive invasive surgery is being replaced by new techniques and equipment. Ultra-sound waves can be used to destroy diseased tissue. Microsurgery, using computer-guided scalpels, is already dealing efficiently with various complicated situations in our internal organs. Eventually new automation could provide remote-control surgery. According to scientists at the Massachusetts Institute of Technology, in eight to ten years' time micro-robots as thin as paper-clips will be able to crawl into our bodies to carry out surgery. They will be small enough to be used in the ear canal, for example.

Fourthly, and perhaps most importantly, there is the mystery of the whereabouts of the mind, or soul. According to Francis Crick, who, with James Watson, shared a Nobel prize for the discovery of the DNA molecule, it lies in the brain. It is an entity, he claims, which 'is the rich result emerging from the interaction of billions of the brain's nerve cells . . . This does not deny the soul or belittle our values, but it does place the soul within our heads . . . Only scientific certainty can in the long run rid us of the superstitions of our ancestors.'

In all of this I would not want any reader to think I am claiming to be some sort of superman. My annual medical report for my ninetieth year told me it was too late to replace my worn-out artificial hip joints, which had been inserted in a double operation more than two decades earlier, when I was sixty-nine. It emerged that the surgeons might still have been able to do something for me when I was eighty-five; now the risk of things going wrong was too high. So, I asked them, why hadn't they done anything five years earlier? 'We never thought you'd live so long,' they replied. The outcome is that I still manage on a couple of sticks – the original pair I was given in 1974!

The risk centred on one main point, the doctors went on to explain. My immune system was in balance, and even the anaesthetic would be enough to divert some of its protective qualities to combat the new invader, so allowing other enemies, currently being kept at bay, to break through my defences. This idea of balance had never occurred to me before, but it seemed to contain an echo of the ancient concept of the body's four elements – earth, air, fire and water – and of the mind's four humours – the sanguine, choleric, phlegmatic and melancholic. For centuries it was believed that failures in physical and mental health could be explained by these being put out of balance. Now the idea of balance returned full circle in the most up-to-date scientific explanations for our states of body and mind.

Certainly I would never claim to have a better than average constitution. The facts are that my father and mother were orphans. Of the seven aunts and uncles who welcomed my birth, only two were still here to see my fifth birthday. I suffered from asthma, bronchitis and pneumonia and had no appetite. When I was six, to improve my chances of survival, my parents moved from Belfast to live by the sea at the Northern Ireland resort of Bangor. There I gradually recovered my appetite and grew stronger. Within a year I had begun to run round the sea front each morning and was swimming in the sea winter and summer. In the garden I rigged up a climbing rope, a trapeze and weights. At nine I was sent to Campbell College, a boarding school, and there found that I enjoyed boxing, fencing, rugby and athletics.

In India, at the age of twenty-three, I suffered three bouts of malignant malaria, one of which almost proved fatal and left me slightly deaf from the quinine treatment. Two years later a bad fall from a horse damaged my spine and forced me to wear, from time to time, a surgical corset and a cervical collar. Over the years, the condition gradually worsened, leading eventually to my double hip-joint replacement operation. Today I manage very well by using my two sticks for walking and wheelchairs for airports and museums, but my main support has been the hour a day I spend exercising in a swimming pool. This has kept my body toned up without causing further injury to the loose joints. When it came to my ninetieth birthday, friends remarked on how well I looked and spoke. 'How have you lived so well?' they asked. This book is my answer.

5

Love and Sex

Love makes the world go round. It is selfless and unde-
manding; or it should be, if we are using the word in the
correct sense. 'Love thy neighbour as thyself.' Sex is a
mating dance: you have to learn to dance to reward your
partner. It is nature's solution to ensure the survival of the
species, the surge of animal attraction that assails the animal
kingdom. The chief component of this attraction appears
to be smell. This is how animals find their mates; how lambs
distinguish their mothers in a herd of sheep; how snakes
find their partners, and prey, by using their forked tongues
to scent 'chemical footprints' left on the ground. It is how
animals claim and protect their territory; it is the way in
which moths are attracted to mates over distances of several
miles. For the queen bee, smell is the dominant feature of
her control over her 60,000 subjects in the hive.

The human animal has, in its civilized state, lost much of
its sense of smell, which was formerly essential to survival, as
we may see from the example of the bushmen who can

smell water many leagues away in the desert. Subliminally, however, a sense of smell still accounts for much in matters of attraction between the sexes. To replace what has been lost in sensitivity to natural scents, we have devised our own attractive substitutes. Perfumes have been used by women since at least the days of Ancient Egypt, when the ladies wore on their heads cones of scented wax which gradually melted and perfumed them as the evening progressed. Today perfumes for men are gaining in popularity.

But, quite apart from projecting our smell, it is my belief that each of us is also surrounded by an invisible aura that is in the nature of a magnetic field. This field appears to interact with the magnetic fields of everyone else we meet, helping us to evaluate a situation, like a radar scan at sea. As a hypothesis it helps to account for those occasions when we feel immediate attraction and sympathy for someone we have never met before, or a sense of repulsion, or simply experience a negative, indifferent reaction. It is a process which some would call psychic in the occult sense, but it seems far more likely that it relates to a faculty of the unconscious mind. By paying attention to it, we may sharpen our sensitivity to other people; and maybe it can help to save us from making mistakes in our emotional lives.

In the immobile vegetable kingdom, insects often provide a substitute for animal intercourse. How are they encouraged to perform this function? Again, a sense of smell is the key. Plants attract insects by the sweet-scented nectar in their flowers. The male element, pollen, is carried by the insects and attaches itself to the ovules of the female flowers, thus fertilizing the seeds of the plant. Some plants have flowers which smell like rotting meat, and this attracts flies that perform the same fertilizing function. The relationship of mutual advantage, called symbiosis, is a pointer towards the reality of the natural laws of evolution: the plant is fertilized and the insect gains the nectar. Some plants, such as the Venus fly-trap, attract insects under false pretences and consume them. Nature is rich in metaphors for the human condition.

Therefore we may well ask ourselves whether it is worth while to get tangled up in the tender trap of love, whose central goal is the production of children for the survival of the species. Babies are not for Christmas; they will be there until death takes over. Is it worth the prospect of a lifetime of worry and responsibility to add to the population of an already overcrowded planet on which people are living longer than ever before and machines are systematically replacing manual labour? Before long, most of us are going to have to learn how to spend and enjoy a large quantity of leisure – another problem for our educational system, which our governments have as yet hardly begun to address.

Boredom, as may already be witnessed in a multitude of examples around, can be a dangerous source of social disturbance and crime. In China I saw vast gangs of men and women cutting embankments through hills and digging huge reservoirs, equipped only with buckets and spades. Chinese officials told me how essential it was for the country to catch up with the West and obtain giant earth-shifting machines to relieve this manual burden. 'And when that happens, what will the present workers do?' I asked. They could give me no practical reply. More recently there have been signs in China of a rising crime rate moving beyond the ability of its authoritarian government to control it.

If the world population were to be halved, there would be plenty for all, combined with a high level of employment and a freedom from much drudgery. Achieving this, on the other hand, would require a change of heart on the part of religious leaders who need followers, and dictators who need cannon fodder. In the United Kingdom, our present population stands at over 57 million and is projected to exceed 59 million by the year 2000. Addressing the First

World Optimum Population Congress, held at the University of Cambridge in August 1993, David Richardson, a former marine biologist, was quoted in *The Times* as saying: 'At the moment we have a congested society. The scientific evidence is that at 30 million [for the UK] we get relief on resources, many more people would be employed and we would have the basis for a healthier society.' Provided a fertility rate of 1.8 remained constant, a population of 30 million could be achieved in 150 years. Taxation policies to encourage small families could then maintain this figure into the future. Setting out to achieve this target would provide a lead to developing nations whose populations are booming out of control. The world's population now stands at about 5,500 million, with 98 million new lives being added each year. The United Nations has estimated that, by 2050, the global population could reach 12,500 million.

Also in August 1993, *The Times* predicted that the then forthcoming papal encyclical, *Veritatis Splendor*, would make it clear 'that Catholics must accept as infallible the Church's strictures that sex must have procreation as its ultimate end and that contraception was against nature'. Since there are some 900 million Catholics in the world population, those who are not of the Catholic faith may thank their lucky stars that a gulf appears to exist between the Pope and many of his flock. As Peter Stanford, a former editor of the *Catholic Herald*, wrote in the *Independent on Sunday* of 15 September 1993:

Not only are individual Catholics making their own minds up on issues such as contraception, remarriage and homosexuality, but priests, bishops, theologians and even cardinals are publicly questioning the papal line . . .

An opinion poll, published on the eve of his [the Pope's] visit to the United States last week, revealed the abyss between America's 59 million Catholics and their leader. According to the survey, 84 per cent opposed the Vatican's ban on the Pill . . . Even on abortion, once the keystone of orthodoxy, 58 per cent rejected a total ban.

In Western Europe, too, Catholics are ignoring the Pope's holy writ and following their own consciences . . . continuing to attend mass, receive communion and take their chances on Judgement Day.

The original purpose of sex in season in the animal kingdom was to give a species the best possible chance of survival. In the human animal, the seasonal aspect of mating fell away when it ceased to be necessary. In evolutionary terms, however, our new dilemma has come upon us with abrupt speed and demands the use of our rational faculties, for again the question is one of survival. A world of uncontained population growth is clearly a world that threatens not only the lives of an immeasurable number of individuals but also the very continuance of *Homo sapiens*. Women have been programmed by nature for millions of years to produce children for the survival of the species. In the wild state, animal populations rise or fall according to the amount of food available. Today, nature's method of population control does not in general apply to humans. Food is given to drought-ravaged areas and people leave their stricken farms for food encampments. Here, though they have access to food, they are still left with no occupation and despair in their hearts; and so nature encourages them to breed afresh so that the tribe may be perpetuated. Then, when the emergency has ended, it is not easy for them to return to pick up the threads of their original lifestyle, especially since there will by now be even more children to feed.

In a situation in which millions are born to little hope of a decent life, we may expect Mother Nature to take her unsentimental way with us. Already many diseases that we thought our ingenuity had confined to the dustbin of history are returning in new virulent forms, waiting on the sidelines for the day when antibiotics and other defences falter in their effectiveness. The wars of the present day, mostly to do with territory for ethnic or religious groups, could well evolve into the far more terrifying prospect of wars to secure exclusive global control of dwindling precious resources, of which water is only one of the foremost examples.

The advantages of population limitation are so obvious, in other words, that, unless we destroy all the inhabitants of the planet in a global war that sees the unleashing of our weapons of mass-destruction, then the day must surely dawn when a reduced population enjoys peace and everything it requires. Then our descendants will at least have time to remember what most of us have forgotten: that the only things on earth which really matter are such imponderables as beauty and wisdom, laughter and love.

In China, India and Singapore, various methods to control birth-rates have been tried, but in many other countries custom, dictators and religion continue to demand large families. In such societies the woman is still a fertility symbol, as she was in France after the Second World War. I once attended a ceremony where the French mayor presented gold medals to mothers with ten children, silver medals to those with nine and bronze to those with eight. Looking at the bronze medalists, it was plain to see they intended going for gold.

The future stability of certain nations is being challenged by the rapid increase of minority groups. High birth-rates are among the tactics being used by various shades of fundamentalists to further their dangerous causes in established and emergent liberal democracies. It is to be hoped that education will continue the process of freeing women around the world from being little more than breeding machines for power-driven authorities, and bring recognition at this late hour of their right to equality. In many countries they are already equal in theory, and household chores are increasingly shared by men, who are also encouraged to be with their wives during the births of their children. This *is* a positive indicator of progress; such a thing was unheard of in my day. Men and women should indeed be equal partners, and help each other to face life's trials and adventures undaunted. We can afford nothing less. The time has gone for the old taboos. There should be no segregation, no second-class citizenship. In any case, advanced technology has given women the upper hand over men. Physical strength is no longer the key to dominance. Furthermore, men no longer exercise key decisions over the births of children; this has become the woman's choice.

All of this leaves us, on the other hand, with a confusion of attitudes to human sexuality which the alienations within society do little to help. Casual sex avoids or dodges the creative use of sex to build lasting relationships – the process of bonding that is its most important function after creating children. It therefore logically becomes the most important function of sex in a world in which children are already over-plentiful. Single-parent families have doubled in the United Kingdom during the past ten years, and their proportion continues to increase. In Sweden, over half of all families are single parent. This trend is in part the result of pregnancies in teenagers and young unmarried women, in part the result of an increasing incidence of breakdowns in mutual commitment between young couples. In either instance it is, as a rule, the mothers who are left holding the babies. Whatever the causes, no one could possibly claim that it represents anything that could remotely be described as socially desirable.

It is to be hoped that direct education in the realities of sexual consequences and parenthood will, in the long run, alleviate this situation. Skilful education of children in a knowledge of sex and human biology at the right stages undoubtedly helps to cultivate mature attitudes. It all comes down to giving young people a prospect of wider and richer options. There can be no advantages to society in having a large proportion of a whole generation of babies being born to young (sometimes very young) single mothers, who may instinctively feel that this is the only way they can bring a meaningful or rewarding relationship into the orbit of their own lives.

The freedoms and tolerance abounding today are in danger of becoming as great a social tyranny as the old prohibitions used to be. The pill has allowed girls to claim the same freedom as boys; the demand for female equality has removed a protective layer on which women could formerly rely. Hence the growing number of one-parent families and the readiness of couples to go their own ways, breaking up the parental unit when their children have most need of it. The adult children, in turn, then leave their parents to moulder away in nursing and rest-homes in their old age, and become too busy and preoccupied with their own affairs ever to visit them – the lack of love that makes the world go round.

Sex has its importance. Taken on its own, in isolation, however, it is not love any more than possessiveness, manipulation and emotional blackmail are love. We can also observe around us many evidences for the way in which the enormous power of sex is used in negative ways, to humiliate, hurt, dominate and exact submission. An under-current of rape, sexual sadism and murder runs through many strata of life today, and society seems at a loss to know what can be done to control it. Violence against women, especially in a domestic setting, perhaps represents a primitive response within certain male psyches to the fact that women today proclaim their right to independent choice – a crude attempt to reassert male supremacy.

Meanwhile nature's law of the survival of the fittest has been hijacked and distorted by military warlords, a prime example being the so-called 'ethnic cleansing' and slaughter of the innocents in the former Yugoslavia. The rape of women has here gone side by side with the extreme cynical tactic of using civilians, and even UN peacekeepers, as shields and hostages to the fortunes of war. Fundamentalists have hijacked religion with similar terrible results. All it is possible to say is that any cause which feels it has to use rape and hostage-taking must, by definition, be morally bankrupt. It seems unlikely that matters will improve until man begins to use his brain to replace faith and pseudo-mystical notions of nationalism with fact.

The oldest profession in the world catered, as it still does, for many shades of sex. History is filled with famous whores, including Mary Magdalen. Concubines and harems supplied the needs of the wealthy and powerful; the poor found comfort in red-light areas. The most renowned houses of pleasure were those of Paris, and they attracted the whole world. Here sex was presented with a combination of elegance and erotic fantasy unmatched in any other country, but eventually these establishments suffered closure after a woman was elected to the French Senate. Bangkok succeeded Paris as the sex capital of the world, and the package-tour industry was soon taking plane loads of sexual athletes of every persuasion there to add further trophies to their sexual marathons.

Shortly after the war, when I was producing *Street Corner*, a documentary film about London's policewomen, their commandant Betty Bather told me that London prostitutes performed a useful job by simply listening to their clients' troubles. For many men, payment obtained them sex without guilt; they felt free to talk, to expose their most secret fantasies and discuss more serious problems. Prostitutes could in effect become well-qualified counsellors. Many deserved recognition for the counsel and comfort they gave to men who were deformed or disturbed, and therefore regarded as 'odd'. In the bedroom their money was as good as the next man's; they became equal. It seems to be a necessary safety-valve. Any developed society that lacks this source of sex comfort – offering sex as therapy – will almost certainly see increases in attacks on women and girls.

On a personal level between the sexes, marriage remains the most exacting contract of all. In my youth it was the only career prospect available to a majority of girls, and predatory mamas set off in hot pursuit of eligible bachelors. My mother used to tell me and my brother an old Irish proverb that compared the lottery of marriage to a man plunging his arm into a sack of a hundred serpents and an eel. Question: 'If he manages to catch the eel without being bitten, what has he got?' Answer: 'Just a wet fish.' Today, in many developed and developing countries, every career is open to both sexes, and women have proved themselves to be as capable as men, and sometimes considerably more competent. Recently they have come into films and television to perform tasks that would never have been dreamed of as suitable for women during my day in those industries; they receive equal credits, and quite right too. Marriage is no longer the only career on the horizon, and the biological clock for child-rearing has extended into later life, thus allowing bright and intelligent women to enjoy careers as well as children. Their potential range of ability is not, as was once the case, lost to society.

And still nature draws lovers together to ensure the continuity of the species. With the arrival of children, nature transforms lust to mother-love in the woman, for the survival of the children becomes the paramount issue. The husband may resent this fact, and should his wife then fail to include him in the new grouping as the most important member of the family, he may set off in search of a new and more understanding mate – only to find the process repeating itself. Men beware! Multiple marriages are on the increase.

Husband and wife share the history of their lives, and this valuable piece of living is unfortunately lost with any change of partner. The loss entailed does not prevent more than 60 per cent of Californian marriages ending in divorce. Fortunately, however, it is never too late to join up with the right partner. A shared experience doubles the joy and halves the sorrow.

So where does all of this leave us where love is concerned? Love is for laughter, for loving others, for the joy that may be defined as the art of living. In this the values of marriage as a basis for partnership seem likely to reassert themselves for a new generation, as part of a natural cycle – but freed from the old judgemental rule on which they once depended. The actress Mrs Patrick Campbell expressed a point of view on this process when she described her marriage as being like 'the deep, deep peace of the double-bed after the hurley-burley of the chaise-longue'.

Sex can and should be a great source of comfort and joy to the elderly. The idea that after fifty it no longer matters, and that people should neglect it for 'higher' pursuits, is ridiculous. Cuddling and intimacy are more important in old age, when real intimacy of body and mind reaches a new level of importance, no longer involved with a youthful erection in search of nubile young women. Many elderly men and women who have strong sexual desires are overcome by feelings of guilt and shame, and feel they must be over-sexed. This is silly. The old should rejoice in their libido, and lusty old men should be presented with medals.

The onset of coronary problems, cancers and other potentially fatal conditions provide the opportunity for reality and truth to be strengthened as a part of honest love for one's partner. And here, too, sex has an important part to play. As the ancient Chinese said, 'As long as a man can close his hand he can make love.'

6

People and Friendship

'Hell is other people,' wrote the French philosopher and author Jean-Paul Sartre. Without other people it would be impossible for us to prove our existence. In the view of the existential philosophers, we exist only in relation to others. To say that we were alone at the time of a crime does not constitute an alibi. Each individual is unique; each has a long history of personal survival. Survival is our strongest instinct; threatened people can become dangerous. Those who are the worse for drink or drugs are all the more likely to behave violently or dangerously as a distorted instinct overrides rational judgement.

All of this being so, how best to enjoy other people? First, it is as well to consider the number of friends a person may hope to be able to sustain at any one period in their lifetime. As genetic research has shown, our nearest relatives among the primates are chimpanzees, and their communal groups vary between twenty and twenty-five. This is the population size that enables them to bond by mutual grooming and other activities. A larger group would not be able to bond and hold together as a group.

The brain size of a chimpanzee is one-sixth that of a human brain. Using this comparison as a yardstick, a human should have a capacity to sustain personal association with between 120 and 150 fellow-humans. This conjecture is supported by various phenomena, including such facts as that our ancestors lived in groups of about 150, while the largest independent unit in a modern army remains a company of between 130 and 150 soldiers. In a larger grouping than this it would cease to be possible to run a fighting unit on a person-to-person basis, and there would be a dangerous loss of efficiency. The same applies to commercial business units. Small is beautiful. Expansion can bring disaster unless it is properly controlled to allow sufficient independence in each division or sector.

Friends may be defined as those rare people who help one another when the need arises. Chimpanzees rely on a similar attitude of mutual co-operation. But leaders of religion, presidents, prime ministers, people in positions of power and dictators will be lucky if they have any real friends. Their tribes are too large to grant them such blessings. Their subjects are ruled by various grades of fear, from the fear of being left out to the fear of punishment. The price that leaders and the very rich pay for their eminence is isolation and haunting suspicions of the motives of those around them who claim to be their friends. The Saddam Husseins of this world sometimes even have to resort to shooting their friends should they develop doubts about their loyalty; only then can they sleep easily in their beds!

Modern discontent arises from people losing their sense of belonging to a community, of being part of a network of personal relations, and becoming instead little more than a number in the records of social security computers. This is the greatest change which any of us have had to face during the twentieth century. The close-knit villages of my youth, where everyone knew everyone else and had a well-defined space in a small society, have lost much of that quality. There is far more of a feeling that our lives are in the hands of advisers and civil servants, detached from the real world, who play games with numbers. We feel we are at the mercy of political leaders and legislators whose aim too often seems to be to outwit rather than work with the democratic process. Too many policy decisions and pieces of legislation pass into law under hasty political pressure without their consequences having been properly thought through. Philosophy has been downgraded; the centralized authorities have the final say. At the end of the day, it is history alone that has something of value to teach us, but this, because of a lack of practical education, has been deprived of much of its potential to help our understanding of the world. The pressures of vested interests, prejudice and unwillingness to carry out the necessary work result in a flight from reason which leads people to seek refuge in religious fundamentalism, for it often seems that we cannot go forward without going back.

In 1905, the fashion was still for large families. My father was one of eight, but by the time I was five years old only two of his siblings remained alive. At the start of my life I shared the planet with 1,500 million others. The world population today is four times larger and, as we have seen, is growing rapidly. Overcrowded humans, like overcrowded animals, have taken to killing each other on the slightest provocation. Fear is one of the deadliest ingredients in the soup of hatred. 'Ethnic cleansing' is the new term coined to describe the terrorizing of innocent people where they must face either being murdered or driven from a territory because of their religion, nationality or social group. In a world awash with lethal weaponry, the individual life has become cheap in the eyes of terrorist, mugger, drugs gangster and irregular militiaman alike.

We need to stop here and redefine the essentials for

living. I suggest that these two are among the most important: first, unlimited compassion, and second, unlimited persistence in uncovering the reality of any situation. Once the reasons for other people's actions have become crystal clear, then at least a situation holds out the hope of being resolved. Misunderstanding a situation can, on the other hand, lead to years of trouble. Before the onslaught of the Gulf War, Saddam Hussein felt secure in his project for Iraq to take over Kuwait by force. The West had supplied him with arms and been unclear in its signals, leaving him confident that it would never, if it came to a showdown, go to war over the issue. As we know, he was disastrously mistaken. A few years earlier, the leaders of the Argentine junta had similarly been lulled into the belief that, if it came to the reality of an invasion of the Falkland Islands, then Britain would rather write them off than fight to retain them. In fact Britain gathered its resources to fight.

It was Mother Nature who brought us into the world. Under her laws we crawled out of the seas and reached towards the stars. Along the way we have found out some of her secrets in her tactics for controlling the ebb and flow of life on earth. On the plains of Serengeti, for instance, many species of animals have survived for 50 million years without assistance from humans, their numbers rising or falling in harmony and balance with the amount of food available. Humans, being too clever by half, have meanwhile overturned nature's control and produced food in abundance and themselves in super-abundance. We are now ourselves the greatest threat to the wonderful variety of life. Our beautiful planet is polluted with our garbage, which accumulates even in some of the remotest corners of surviving wilderness. Its rich resources are being laid waste by greed and the ever-increasing demands of the human race as it expands at the rate of 200,000 new mouths a day.

Nature programmed people to have children. Millions

of eggs and billions of sperm are produced daily in the race for survival. But her control system, the death of the unfit and of those who eat the seed corn, is unacceptable to modern society, which feels that it should technically be feasible to produce a world of plenty for all. Again, unless we face up to the realities of population control, we shall squander all the gains we have made through knowledge and science. We are already poised on the ledge of an abyss of social breakdown because of the pressures of scale represented by ever-growing numbers. It may be that the only solution lies in restoring a natural balance between our human population and the conditions needed for the planet to remain viable; otherwise it may turn out that the planet itself ejects us and sets about putting itself to rights. This is a fate that could seem to be fully deserved, but Arthur C. Clarke has stated the optimistic alternative in his Foreword to a collection of his essays and speeches, *1984: Spring – A Choice of Futures*: 'Apocalypse may yet be cancelled; let us dare to be hopeful.'

To achieve this optimistic outcome it will be necessary for each country to reach agreement on a population limit consonant with both protecting the environment and providing a quality of life for its citizens. It will also need to guard against the possibility, already mentioned, of one sector within a community using more intensive breeding as a tactic to create its own dominant élite, so gaining cultural and political control over the population in general. How, then, are we to control breeding? It can only be done through education in the problem and rewarding those who agree to live by the implications.

As matters stand, far too many cars use the roads in and around central London and the much-vaunted democratic freedom of the individual motorist becomes a tyranny that is destroying lifestyle and air quality for tens of thousands of fellow-citizens and threatening the health of children. A new system of licensing or control to limit road use is therefore inevitable in the near future, and probably over-due. Thinking along parallel lines, a country might consider a licence to have children. After all, at present-day money values in the United Kingdom, they each cost £100,000 to raise to maturity and can turn out to be even more dangerous than motor-cars! The freedom to enjoy can also be the freedom to destroy. As a further illustration of this we need only think of the way in which the hordes of tourists, as they go about the globe, destroy by their pressure of numbers whatever qualities they are searching for in a place.

The overcrowding of the earth with people has led to the question of whether we might colonize another planet and so fulfil the science-fiction visions of writers like Ray Bradbury in his *Martian Chronicles*. Living in space stations is already under trial in the United States, but so far there have been no indications that such a way of life could be successfully sustained for all or the major part of a life-span. Yet, even if it did become technically possible, would such an existence be acceptable? Our leading space experts dismiss the proposal as unlikely. Loren Eisley has written on the prospects of our ever making contact with manifestations of life elsewhere in the universe:

> Nowhere in all space or on a thousand worlds will there be men to share our loneliness. There may be wisdom, there may be power, somewhere across space great instruments may stare vainly at our floating cloud rack, their owners yearning as we yearn. Nevertheless, in the nature of life and in the principles of evolution we have had our answer. Of men elsewhere and beyond, there will be none for ever.

It all boils down to the fact that we are on our own in our search for a solution to our population problem. We have only our own resources and abilities – our own boot straps!

From infancy onwards we are dependent on others – our mother and father, family and neighbours. Frequently these others seem to stand in the way of our young desires, and so we have quarrels with them, in which mother and father are likely to be our first victims. It requires a long process of maturing before we can accept that everyone does what they consider to be best for themselves and for others within their own situations. The attitudes of others may be seen by the world as either selfish or altruistic, but their actions, whichever way they are viewed, still represent what they want to do, and are therefore motivated by self-interest. Mother Teresa and Bob Geldof do what they want to do; thus their self-interest becomes productive for others. National political or religious leaders, whether they are operating in systems that are democratic or authoritarian, still similarly convince themselves that whatever they do is best for their people, even if they are simply pursuing their own notions and ambitions.

The Sufi, a mystical order within Islam, have often used teaching stories to illustrate reality. These parables convey profound wisdom with instant impact. Here is a couple of samples:

A tortoise carries a stranded scorpion across a river. On reaching the farther bank the scorpion stings the tortoise, who indignantly demands: 'My nature is to be helpful. I have helped you and now you sting me.' 'My friend,' replies the scorpion, 'your nature may be to be helpful, but mine is to sting. Why do you seek to transform your nature into a virtue and mine into a villainy?'

An elephant and a mouse fell in love. On their wedding night the elephant collapsed and died. 'Oh Fate!'

lamented the mouse. 'I have unknowingly bartered one moment of pleasure and tons of imagination for a lifetime of digging a grave.'

It is difficult to see how the personal, instinctive programming to reproduce, built into everyone's survival systems for millions of generations, can ever be altered. But, unless it changes, the chances of humanity surviving grow ever more slender. Continuing the battle for supremacy has failed to bring peace and prosperity. Hardly a day goes by without fearful examples of man's inhumanity to man flaring up like bush fires in one part of the world or another. Each outbreak seems almost impossible to extinguish, and each creates a further legacy of bitterness to be carried forward into future generations and exploited by ruthless politicians. The violence subsides in one area only to erupt in another. We have all seen the daily newspaper reports of the horrors and atrocities endured by the peoples of Africa, of the Balkans, of my own country, Ireland. The response of everyone is to pay lip-service to wanting to see peace on earth, but this happy situation, if it ever arrives, will not be a reality for many generations.

There have been innumerable experiments to create a utopia on earth, among which communism has been the most extensive in its geographical and political influence. It has also been the most spectacular failure, involving cynicism, oppression and cruelty. The politician Chris Patten, the last British Governor of Hong Kong, defined it in an article in *The Times* of 30 July 1993 as 'one of this century's ghastly attempts to impose Heaven on Earth by brutal centralism and suppression of individualism. Like other efforts it failed horribly because of those who opposed it and partly because of its own lunacies and internal contradictions.'

Individual needs and interests are fundamental to the social pattern. I used to give my children an example of this on our visits to the zoo, where we instantly recognized that different animals have different needs: monkeys like nuts, lions don't; some animals show off, others sulk. People are the most sophisticated of all animals and require the greatest care and consideration in any approach. As an old saying goes, you catch more flies with honey than with vinegar. It is not a question of liking or not liking people; rather is it a question of appreciating their way of life, whether or not you agree with it. If you can only tolerate people who agree with you, or whose opinions are identical to your own, then you cut yourself off from the reality of a full and rounded life.

There is a difference between clever people and wise people. It is always the wise people, whether or not they are educated in a conventional sense, who will be the greatest help to you. The clever people are more likely to be a hindrance or a liability, as we saw in the parable already told of the three professors in the jungle who resurrected a heap of bones into a live Bengal tiger. So how are we to set about living a full, rewarding and happy life? First we need to wipe our slates clean of all the inbred prejudices and fears encrusted on them by millions of years of survival in a hostile world; then we must start afresh, using the finest gift of nature, the human brain, to test every issue with logic, humility and compassion. Many wise men have left us guidelines. Confucius said: 'Do not do unto others that which you would not like done unto yourself.' Buddha said: 'Be ye lamps unto yourselves, do not rely on others.' Shakespeare said: 'This above all – to thine own self be true; and it must follow as night the day thou canst not then be false to any man.' Jesus said: 'Love your enemies and those that despitefully use you.'

Alas, these profound paths of wisdom are seldom followed in practice. Some of the wise men also had the truths they had uttered 'twisted by knaves to make a trap for fools'. Others were used by vast organizations to gain control over people's lives and consciences. Christian fought against Christian in two world wars. So, what to do? Well, for one thing, enjoy the infinite variety of people and cultures. 'Judge not that ye be not judged.' We all come from the same source. Our common ancestors had the genes we possess today. If only our species manages to survive long enough, then people may at last listen to the words of the wise men and turn to love – the love that will, we have been told, cast out fear.

I have been fortunate in being able to become acquainted with many people in many countries and, during my time as a banker, to have found myself in a position of trust so that a mutual bond was there from the first meeting. I am naturally gregarious; I like people; I have learnt something from everyone; my clients became my friends. It is pointless to go through life weighing up the value of people in terms of wealth, dress, speech, class, colour or creed, and conversing only with your peers. Since life is for living and learning, then it follows that those from every background, no matter how humble, have something of value to contribute.

Friends real and true are those wonderful people with whom, after a separation of twenty years, you pick up where you both left off. As often as not you find there is no need for words between you as you meet again. You and they are in tune. They form a pool of empathy and harmony in which you can relax. At the opposite pole are the spiteful, the bad-tempered, the bad-mannered, the destructive, who seem intent on causing discord. They are the tip of an iceberg of personalities who carry permanent grudges against the world and society. Hate requires a good deal of energy and is a tragic waste of valuable time; it is a negative drive. No professional boxer will waste time in hating his opponent. He knows that his chances of winning depend on his remaining cool and calm and maintaining respect for the skills of his adversary. If he is a genuine sportsman, he will speak well of him, whether he wins or loses.

Emotions are bipolar, opposite ends of the same plank. The mother who snatches her child from the path of a car is also likely to follow the incident through by giving the child a smack as her fear turns to anger. Rejection can turn love back upon itself within the psyche and transform it into hate. As the dramatist William Congreve wrote:

Heaven has no rage, like love to hatred turned,
Nor Hell a fury, like a woman scorned.

Love turning to hate, or vice versa, is something we have often seen in life and fiction. This was the theme of *The Seventh Veil*, a well-known film made soon after the Second World War in which the heroine, played by Ann Todd, finally fell in love with her hated music master, played by James Mason. Families are no strangers to love and hate, but the majority accept these ups and downs as the payment due for the privilege of the overall comfort of being able to live among essentially caring people.

It is important to cultivate a wide range of friends. A common mistake of the elderly is to allow themselves to become trapped in the narrow age band of their own generation. Better to stay in touch with, and open to, the views of the young, and you and they will be amply rewarded. 'If a man does not make new acquaintance as he advances through life,' said Dr Samuel Johnson, as James Boswell recorded in his distinguished biography, 'he will soon find himself left alone. A man, Sir, should keep his friendship in constant repair.'

I am particularly lucky in possessing a library of the photographs I have taken throughout my life in every sphere of work and travel. Today I am approached by picture researchers, mostly young and enthusiastic, who are searching for a specific subject for their art editors. I talk to them about the purpose of the photograph, and sometimes they decide that a better effect would be gained from quite a different picture from the one they came in search of. But, knowing editors only too well, I then suggest that they take away prints illustrating both viewpoints, so that the most suitable can be chosen. At the end of the day, everyone is then likely to be happy – and I am happy above all, since I have been supplied with stimulating conversation and discussion.

There is a recent phenomenon called 'ageism' which sometimes turns into a positive hostility towards the old, or even the not so old. Its motto seems to be, 'Move over, this is a young man's world.' The Chinese, who venerate age, have no such problems. The attitude of ageism is discounted by two facts alone. The first is that a so-called 'youth culture' is itself limited and parochial in ways that those who are caught in its toils may only perceive as they grow older. The second is that the experience of the older generation is capable of bringing a wider knowledge and experience to the counsel table than could ever be available from any other source. The views of a team of psychologists, reported in *The Times* of 11 April 1992, were that the best years of life belong to the elderly: 'When you are younger you constantly worry about what you are going to achieve. Older people base their judgements about satisfaction on what they have achieved.'

I have to confess that, in the days of my youth, I did not always see eye to eye with my father. His usual response during a disagreement was to say it was impossible to put an old head on young shoulders. As I grew up I was amazed to discover how much he had improved with the years!

7

Entertaining: The Round Table

Entertaining is a most rewarding part of living and a component of friendship. After my death, if I were allowed to
return to earth for a few hours, I would wish for nothing
more than to pass them with friends round our dinner
table. This is where my happiest moments have been spent
with my wife, Betty, and our friends, discussing all manner
of subjects and bringing the whole world into our dining
room. Entertaining is, I believe, an art that flourishes best
in one's own home. Three elements are essential to its
success: the flare or ability to chose the right mix of people,
a round table and the provision of good food and drink.
For Betty and myself these occasions have centred on our
round table. The Round Table of King Arthur has a special
significance in chivalric myth, but every round table pos-
sesses a magic of its own: the guests are equally placed; they
can talk to each other across the table; they can instantly
catch and follow reactions to their conversations.

  Our first round table was a Victorian piece that seated

six. It rested on a single pedestal, and no table legs therefore divided our guests. Nor did we ever leave the table until the party came to its natural end. Leaving the table, we found, broke the magic circle and the comfortable atmosphere was irretrievably lost. As our family grew, I purchased a table with a greater circumference. It, too, was set on a single pedestal, and around it we sometimes managed to seat fourteen at Christmas time. At first Betty thought that this table was going to be too big when there were only the two of us at home, but we found it ideal for spreading out the morning papers and never tired of its welcoming expanse. It promoted conversation, and under its benign influence no subject seemed too difficult to tackle. We continued to learn more grouped around our table than we did in any other situation, and guests often remarked on the way it stimulated their own thoughts and encouraged them to bare their feelings. It brought the shy and reticent into the foreground, while those accustomed to dominate a gathering found they did not have everything so much their own way as usual.

The food served up at the table needs to be as interesting as the guests. By this I do not necessarily mean strange or exotic dishes, but portions made from the best and freshest of available produce, celebrating the bounty of nature and mankind's ability to make it palatable in various ways. Betty would always bake our own bread, and this, served with fresh butter, was invariably warmly welcomed. There is a mystique in breaking bread with friends that you certainly cannot achieve with a sliced loaf from the supermarket. The vegetables came from our garden; a large deep freezer held our surplus summer crops till the following year's were ready; the excellent local butcher and fishmonger helped us to pick from the best stock on their counters. On the subject of how to choose the best meat, Betty had sought the advice of the revered French gastronome André Simon, when we were on our honeymoon in Bordeaux. 'My dear,' he said, 'never buy the piece that the animal uses for running or scratching.'

Excellent cheeses at the right stage for eating, fresh fruit, puddings, coffee, liqueurs and chocolates – all these featured at our board. Wine was another area ripe for exploration, and we served the wines we found we liked ourselves. Our daughter Jane, the wine correspondent to *The Times*, says she considers she owes her knowledge of wine to the early start she got off to at the MacQuitty round table.

But the round table also meant people, another most important part of living. I stopped sending Christmas cards during the Second World War because I came to the conclusion that it would be preferable to talk to my friends over the phone if there was no chance of meeting up. An additional bonus from this decision, of course, was the saving of wood pulp, hence of trees. Christmas cards can make good decorations and be an impressive show of popularity, but most of them tend to leave one none the wiser as to the real situation of the sender. On one occasion, after I had received the usual 'Happy Christmas' card from an old friend, I phoned him only to discover that he was suffering from a terminal illness, had mortgaged his home and invested all his money in an annuity to bring his wife an income. This was a bad enough tale of disaster, but, to top it all, the insurance company with whom the annuity was taken out had then gone bankrupt. Now the bank was poised to foreclose on his house. In the midst of this crisis, however, there was one important source of support that he had overlooked, and fortunately I was able to remind him of it and the matter was successfully resolved.

The older one grows and the longer one survives oneself, then the more inevitable it becomes that friends should either die or vanish into some unfamiliar address, which as likely as not turns out to be a nursing home or, as they are called in China, a 'dying house'; or alternatively, as the current ghastly vernacular phrase has it, one of 'God's waiting rooms'. To these fellow-survivors a weekly phone call will give enormous pleasure. They are the ones who have sat at your 'round table' as you have sat at theirs. Therefore grapple them to you with 'hoops of steel'. They are the fabric of your life; never mind the difficulties. They may have become grumpy rather than grateful, but it could be your turn tomorrow. Talk about the old days and arrange to see each other. Do not wait until the obituaries remind you that it is too late. When they depart it will seem as if they have taken a bit of you with them, as you will also seem to do for those who remain after you. This is no cause for lament; simply a matter of tribute. But it must be a sorrowful thing indeed to depart and leave no sense of an unfilled space.

The unfilled space is empty because the deceased was important and valued, a friend who mattered. Every morning the papers are filled with news of the world's dead. We glance sadly through the roll-call, and every now and then are shocked to discover a report of the passing of someone we have known. But it is the relatives who suffer most, and they as well as ourselves need to take comfort in the fact that, the deeper the sense of loss, the more it shows the joy that was there for all of us in the life just over.

Everything that has gone before is still in place, fixed in its position in time. In the same way, all the people you have known remain a part of you. The heartache will slowly pass, though the pang may take months, even years to fade. There is inevitably an element of selfishness in this process, and we may find it useful to think of practical or emotional ways of supporting the bereaved family, or making a gift to a cause for which the deceased felt a strong commitment.

It is right that we should grieve; wrong to try to bury that grief. It is by our grief that we absorb and honour the life that has been. If we fail to grieve we run the danger of diminishing or even of injuring ourselves.

8

Leisure and Work

Use of leisure will be a top priority in the future as machines
and science take over the operation of more and more of
manufacturing and administrative jobs in factories, banks
and offices. Already lasers, jumbo jets, cellular phones and
automation make it possible to provide, with minimum
labour, many of the needs of advanced countries. The speed
of these developments means they will also have an early
impact in the developing countries. The communication
of ideas will continue to become more user-friendly. Voice-
activated computers will simplify the control of these marvellous machines, and the much-vaunted Internet is only
the start of vast changes in communication that will soon
be commonplaces around the globe. A new generation of
children is already adept at playing a multitude of advanced
computer games and growing up 'computer literate'. It is
only a small further step for them to be using these skills
in all kinds of applications in productive processes.

Unfortunately our educational system has largely failed

to prepare the present generation for the coming revolution in patterns of employment and it is doubtful whether the succeeding generation will be any better ready to cope. People feel they have no purpose in life unless they can find a job to give them dignity and standing; they feel that to lack a job is to be deprived of a birthright. Heavy manufacturing industry is fading, but whole local communities have been conditioned to see or imagine no other possibilities for occupation, wherever they may happen to live. Among the questions the situation raises are these: Who will create the wealth to allow for leisure? How is this wealth to be distributed? How is individual energy and ambition to be channelled for social good? How are boredom and purposelessness to be avoided? So far as the last question is concerned, some of the appalling effects of precisely this situation are already manifest. All these questions need to be addressed with the utmost urgency, however, and there is as yet little sign of it happening.

On the other hand, there are various hopeful signs to set against the pessimistic trend. While traditional forms of employment will inevitably decrease in the labour-intensive industries as the new machines take over, there will be a corresponding increase in service industries. An example of this is provided by Disney World in France, which employs 11,000 people, whereas the total number of electric-power workers in the United Kingdom now amounts to only 7,000.

At the time when I was born, there were some five million people who worked as servants in the United Kingdom. They worked for a whole range of society, from the highest to the lowest in the land. As a modest household, we had the help of a farm girl aged eighteen, who lived in and became a greatly loved member of the family. Her title was 'cook-general', which meant that she assisted my mother with everything – looking after us children, making up the fires, filling and tending the oil-lamps, polishing and cleaning. She was fed and clothed and had her own room, and, in 1905, her wages were twelve gold sovereigns a year. She was like a nightingale in our home, singing as she worked. When she departed from us to get married, we all wept. Even the daughters of titled families also worked in one another's mansions, learning the niceties of high society, maybe even making a match with the son and heir to cement a dynastic union.

Today, of course, service has gone out of fashion. Nevertheless there are good fees to be obtained by those who are willing to adopt a professional approach and pride towards a service vocation. They also have an extra value as rarities; their services are in demand. In the United States a couple acting as butler and housekeeper will be provided with their own well-equipped apartment and car, on top of a salary of around $60,000 a year. In London trained nannies command terms of all found and £150 a week. An efficient trained chauffeur will never be without work, either for individuals or agencies, and domestic service agencies who guarantee high standards in house cleaning find a constant demand for what they offer.

The old-style production lines of manufacturing industry – demeaning, dehumanizing and alienating, as Charlie Chaplin illustrated in his satirical film, *Modern Times* – are becoming a part of history. The mining industry may be in its closing phases, but the dreadful and dangerous working conditions in many old mines of living memory are a thing of the past. The solidarity of the mining communities may have been admirable, but they paid a terrible cost for it. There is a degree of danger in growing sentimental about 'the good old days', for throughout our lives we all have to adjust to change and the fact that nothing remains as it used to be. It is a hard process, and coming to terms with it forms a measure of individual maturity. Theme parks may be useful in giving the young an educational glimpse into their grandparents' and ancestors' lives, but their 'nostalgic' aspect should be treated with caution and the label 'heritage' can be a distorting over-simplification.

At almost every level of society it is no longer possible to think in terms of being trained or educated to perform one specific skill, and then expect that it will guarantee a lifetime of secure employment. The pyramid of occupation is likely, in future, to depend on smaller-scale and more individual, and therefore more self-reliant, activities involving qualities of craftsmanship and ideas. As William Morris said, 'Have nothing in your houses that you do not know to be useful, or believe to be beautiful.' It is desirable to emphasize the transferability and adaptability of skills, both practical and psychological, and the importance of acquiring them in the first place. In this the older generation has already set numerous examples. Up and down the country we hear of retired people saying 'they've never been so busy' as they involve themselves 'creatively' to 'keep their brains active'. They are the backbone of groups and clubs, engaging themselves in local and family history research, conservation, gardening, amateur dramatics and heaven knows what beside. Many even study for Open University degrees at a time in life when the 'ageism' attitude would claim that their usefulness is over.

The 'active elderly' are certainly going to wield political and economic clout in the future, because of the sheer numbers of them surviving to increasingly venerable ages. Anyone who writes them off as an unproductive or acquiescent sector will be making a serious mistake. They will, during the course of their long 'retirements', be poised to enrich the fabric of society in many ways, though not all of these may be obvious or quantifiable in strictly economic terms. Meanwhile those who are of working age will need to accustom themselves to such new ideas a 'flexitime', 'home-working' and other phenomena designed to spread the work market as widely as possible and to utilize work skills from many specializations.

Hobbies are defined as favourite leisure occupations, and as we have seen there is little doubt that there will be abundant leisure for people of all generations in the future. Yet hobbies are not merely recreational, since they can provide continuing, absorbing interests, filling with stimulation or excitement hours which might otherwise be lost. They offer the reward of increasing appreciation in the art of living, and, in this respect, we drastically need to revise our notion of what gives value to us as individuals. We also need to rid ourselves of the idea that leisure is somehow a second-best way of spending time. Perhaps we ought to make up our minds that the time has come to break down the dividing line between activities that we perceive as falling under the headings of work or leisure.

People tend to like what they know rather than to know what they might like if only they tried it. Familiar things are easily accepted, hence the popularity of television, newspapers, music, painting, ballet and opera, all of which have their enthusiastic followers. Each one of these interests, however, is also capable of presenting challenges beyond the range of what is familiar; and in this the religions are no exception. We speak of children needing to be 'stretched' at school; we also ought to welcome being 'stretched' ourselves. Therefore break out of the familiar and explore the unfamiliar; cross boundaries, broaden interests and persevere, until the strange becomes familiar and hopefully in turn offers the pleasure of fresh discoveries. Nothing can be achieved without persistence. The earlier in life one becomes stuck in the tramlines of the familiar, then the harder it will be to shake out of the groove later. To become stuck in the tramlines across the whole range of our attitudes is an unnecessary and unfortunate surrender to the ageing process.

Books can be enjoyed from babyhood; turning picture pages leads on naturally to reading. If the pleasure is imparted at that early stage, then the process becomes free of effort. Book lovers are never short of friends, and they will be friends for all occasions. Readers can carry great minds about in their pocket. Books are a short cut to every interest, every aspect of living. Reading – fiction or non-fiction – is not a passive, unproductive occupation, as earlier generations tended to believe. As we read a book, we recreate what it tells us imaginatively in terms of meaning and image. Reading entertains, but it also feeds our minds, enabling us to interpret and create views of the world and the psychology of living in ways that television seldom achieves. Television dishes up most of its fare ready digested. No wonder despots fear literacy; they would far rather preside over a nation of 'couch potatoes', with all programmes closely controlled. Owners of typewriters in the Romania of the late unlamented President Ceaucescu or the Iraq of Saddam Hussein have been required to register their machines with the state security authorities.

Photography is a hobby that can be rewarding in every sense, including the financial. Cameras have been simplified since I began with them. Point and shoot is all they demand nowadays. The skill lies in the ability to choose a precise instant when a scene and an action present the best picture; the best results will, again, be both an interpretation and a record. Some of the greatest photographers, like Henri Cartier-Bresson or Don McCullin, have a genius for fixing that essential moment in a memorable image. A good still photograph can be worth a thousand words, and captioning pictures may lead on to writing illustrated articles. Anyone who discovers they have something of a flair in this direction can learn. Later on, who knows what opportunities may present themselves – magazines, books, television, films?

When, between the wars, I set out for the Far East to become a banker, I never dreamed or intended that I would ever find myself caught up in such areas as these, but it came about that I worked in all of them. Each one represented an area of self-discovery, and therein lies the key for any of us in finding out of what we are capable. Writing and photography both have the advantage of continuing easily into old age and keeping one actively in the market place. They also promote curiosity and mobility. The good photographer is able to travel wherever he can find interesting subjects. He has an *entrée* to all that is happening, so long as he goes about it with an attitude of tactful reason. People, even top celebrities, like to be photographed and interviewed. The invention of photography has opened a special door to the enjoyment and appreciation of our many-splendoured world. The amateur or the professional photographer can always learn much from visiting photographic exhibitions. Photography is painting with light.

This book does not claim to be anything more than a personal record, so once again we must return to the beginning and ask where it is best to begin. It is for each of us to discover, from the vast range of possibilities, the options that will suit us best. The full enjoyment of the banquet of life is not for lazy people. Those leisure activities that I have found simple to achieve, besides being great fun to do, have been these: gardening, bee-keeping, beer and wine making, and cooking. The rewards of gardening and bee-keeping speak for themselves. Wine and beer kits can produce tolerable or even excellent glasses for sharing with friends, and it is never too late to learn to cook. If you have never cooked before, start by learning how to make a good salad dressing, follow that up with how to cook one good menu, and carry on from there. Many inspired cookery books exist to help you to acquire the craft, but the more you do the more you will develop your own style and approach and become inventive. Do not seek only praise from those who sample your dishes. You need honest criticism as well as appreciation. Who knows but that you may find yourself catering, or cooking for parties, or publishing your own cookery book on the basis of your cooking experiments. At the very least you will end up eating better.

The message is to keep on trying new experiences; to take time to bring variety into your life. The Open University, as I have said, offers endless possibilities and opportunities for study; its purpose is to allow people to fulfil neglected capabilities. Give it a try, and before you know it you may find yourself utterly absorbed. To be able to study a subject in depth is a joy and a satisfaction. In the area of the arts and crafts, too, you can always have a go yourself – drawing, painting, sculpting, weaving, throwing pots. Many great artists have gone unrecognized in their lifetimes, so visit art galleries, auction rooms and studios. You may spot a genius before the rest of the world and do them and yourself a favour by buying some of their work before the prices go through the roof. But never buy work purely with the idea that it will be an investment. That is an approach which will take you down a sterile road, and such calculations can go badly wrong. You should only buy art that you love or that sets off a special instinctive response within yourself, backed by the intention to become informed. Learn to trust your intuitions and never cease to learn.

Never be daunted either by the idea of museums and exhibitions, or put off by the thought of being labelled a 'culture vulture'. Visits to art galleries will show you how famous painters used light. When you go round an art gallery, don't spend time reading descriptions (that can come later), but walk round at a steady pace and look at everything; don't pause in your perambulation until something catches your eye and stops you. Then be like a photographer. First take in the long shot – the establishing shot – and follow it with the mid-shot, concentrating on the main strength of the picture. Finally, zoom in to the close shot, the key element. Then go round again. Use the same method, and soon you will have absorbed what appeals to you most – a visual experience that will become part of your consciousness. Another thing you will discover is that the best paintings have a life of their own. However often you may have seen them before, they will always have something new to offer.

Sport, of course, is another main branch of the leisure tree. Cruel spectator sports, such as bull-fighting, cock-fighting, dog-fighting, badger-baiting or hare-coursing, all of which outrage a sense of kinship with the natural world, are thankfully either being outlawed or replaced by football, tennis, squash, cricket, athletics, snooker and chess, among others. In the end, age will make spectators of us all, but hopefully we will never lose our interest. In the meantime, those who have the urge to participate should enjoy being players while they can still play. The active young may be puzzled at the appeal games like bowls or croquet have for the middle-aged or elderly, but they will discover, when they reach that stage themselves, that these pastimes can continue to be challenging and enjoyable all the way into advanced old age.

In choosing our sport or sports, variety is the spice of life, as it is in all human pursuits. The ambition to excel beyond all others will always take root in certain individuals and lead many of them to become champions in their chosen fields. We can enjoy their exploits, and take pride in their achievements, but most of us need not feel that we have to compete directly. Nowadays, with the decline of the value of 'sportsmanship' and the growth of the 'big money' ethic, their situation does not, in any case, always seem so enviable. World champions in a specific sport have short careers and may in the long-term run into health hazards. They are surrounded by armies of interested helpers and can find little space or time for a happy private life. The fear of losing, or dropping behind, is ever present and creates intolerable pressures. The temptation that they will be able to beat the checks for steroid drugs, taken to enhance development and performance artificially, is always there. In recent years we have seen many examples of young promising athletes in authoritarian countries being subjected to cruelty in training and artificial drug treatments because of the pressures their regimes are under to succeed in the eyes of the world.

Exaggerated competitiveness in sport often means that the games played cease to be sporting. If I sound as if I am being old-fashioned on this topic, then I make no apologies. True sportsmen and women, professional and amateur, will enjoy many different games, whether they win or lose. The skill involved is the essence both of the enjoyment and the satisfaction. Skiing, tennis, golf, swimming, sailing, riding, hill-walking, chess are all among the other activities that can be continued into old age, so try as many as you wish. To round off this chapter I can hardly do better than quote the wisdom of an eminent medical consultant on the risks of inactivity. As Dr Alan Barham Carter has written in his book, *All About Strokes*:

The relationship between activity and stroke incidence is very interesting. When I am asked to see a patient who has had a recent stroke, I am often told by his relatives, 'Well you see doctor I am not surprised – he has been overdoing it.' This is sometimes but not often true; more often I find he has been 'underdoing' it, and by this I mean that a former physically active man has stopped taking his usual exercise. I am no supporter of the theory that exercise is the most important factor in health, and those who make it a god are often immature and difficult people to get on with, but I do know that stopping exercise too early and too completely leads to fat, laziness and a short life for many. Not however for all and many readers will take heart from the words of an old man of ninety whom I saw for a very mild temporary attack of unconsciousness. I asked him how he kept so well and he said, 'I take regular exercise every day of my life – by winding up my watch.'

9

Opportunity

An ancient proverb says: 'There are three things that come not back, the sped arrow, the spoken word and the neglected opportunity.' Of the three, the neglected opportunity is the most devastating. 'If only I had seized my chance,' we lament, kicking ourselves for some irreparable failure to act when the moment was right. So why is it that we let these golden opportunities pass us by, or fail to see them when they are before our eyes? What is it that holds us back from having a go at something new, or blocks our ears to the inner voice that urges us off in fresh directions?

My own view is that the whole nature of formal education provides part of the answer to these questions. Many schools force their pupils into narrow routines and rituals, and they begin to do so at an over-early stage in their lives. The teachers of the present generation have themselves led sheltered existences, growing from pupils into teachers by way of teacher training colleges without ever enduring the tough realities of survival outside the school walls. Many great world leaders were failures at school, including Sir Winston Churchill, and the term often used of them is 'late developers'. Perhaps they were late developers as an instinctive protest against an educational system that sought to pigeonhole and mould them at a pace they sensed was wrong for them as individuals.

The priority of emphasis in measuring the quality of education on offer tends to go by the exam pass rate of students rather than by the extent to which it enhances their potential to end up enjoying useful lives and becoming individually productive by putting their thinking to good use. Young people need to have a positive sense that it is going to be possible for them to contribute to social richness; the tragedy today is that so many of them clearly feel no such thing. A result of this is that their natural tendency towards idealism easily becomes distorted by other forces.

In authoritarian countries schools are obliged to run an educational production line with the objective of turning out fanatics to feed the cause of a religious or political ideology. The pupils unfortunate enough to be caught in such a system become, in effect, victims who discover too late the irreparable loss they have suffered. Much is lost to society of the value of those who can think things through for themselves, but it is also no coincidence that writers, teachers, doctors and other members of the intelligentsia are usually among the first targets of the death squads whenever a new tyranny comes into being.

Yet in democratic societies it also happens that wide areas of interest may be narrowed down to those which lead a student towards simply being top of the class. Then, when other opportunities appear that do not fit the pattern, they are likely to pass unrecognized; or, if they are noticed, they may be dismissed as failing to conform to the mould in which the pupil has been cast. Consider the many examples of the success enjoyed by foreigners, who have arrived in Britain penniless, perhaps speaking only their native language, but who managed over the years to become members of the peerage and leaders of their professions through merit, imagination and work. Such people never allowed themselves to be squeezed into any mould by any educational or political system.

Being a rebel helps. The most valuable lesson education can teach us is how to question received wisdom, and hence how to question within ourselves every assumption we make throughout our lives. If we accept a point of received wisdom, we should do so from a position of freedom, not from one of fear or coercion. Our education should fit us to demand to know the reason for everything, especially when it comes to those duties that teachers require of their students. Advice to the young should run consistently along these lines: develop an inquiring mind and sharpen up your sense of curiosity; discover how things are done to arrive at the end-products for which methods of work aim; consciously grow to be aware of what it is that makes other people tick. It is only through discovering and becoming aware of others that we can discover ourselves.

If all of this is done successfully, then boredom, the great enemy of youth, will be held at bay. In fact it will never become a significant problem in the first place. Today boredom is largely a product of the constant demand for novelty which is both encouraged and exploited by the promoters of a so-called 'youth culture'. It is a state of mind that can drive the personality back upon itself and rob it of the will to act. It is an enemy because it is a negative response which becomes a self-fulfilling prophecy: those who expect to be bored undoubtedly will be bored. In itself boredom positively delays the chances of finding its cure: to set forth along genuine roads of discovery rather than linger in the side-shows of drugs, arcade games and video nasties. In this I am on the side of the young, as we all need to be, for they, with their infinite capacity to see the world afresh, are our future. Unfortunately the more negative aspects often rush in to fill the vacuum in the meantime. The young are more capable of making their own judgements than we give them credit for – if we will only equip them to develop their capacity to think freely.

The quality of teachers who come our way during our educational years is inevitably a game of roulette, and the truly outstanding teacher, who sets the mind alight – who starts us off on a lifetime's exploration – is a *rara avis* at the best of times. Anyone who encounters such a teacher may give thanks for their good fortune. But it is the test of good teachers in general that they will be the ones most likely to encourage a wider view, and therefore those most likely to gain and hold the respect of their students. There is another saying that goes, 'I don't remember what I was taught, I only remember what I learnt.' Even more sceptically, Ananda Cumaraswamy has said, 'It takes four years to get a first-class university education, but it takes forty years to get over it.'

A majority of teachers will always require their students to stick to set books within a curriculum, and government policies today have made it even harder for individually inspiring teachers to exert an influence outside these narrow limits. The best teachers may indeed be those who do not teach in a conventional sense, but who involve their pupils with their own questioning explorations. Such eccentric, unorthodox figures are only too likely to find themselves manoeuvred into early retirement in the context of modern educational pressures.

We need to be clear about one aspect in particular. Advice given to the young should continue along these lines: never narrow your sights to the long-term goals of high position or one specific aspect of an occupation. A broad experience in the earlier stages of any learning process is certain to bring richer rewards in the long term. Too much specialization too soon will set limits on later chances of progress – a principle that applies not only during our school and college years, but throughout our working lives. An initial lack of knowledge of the difficulties in any situation will in fact provide an impetus to deal with them and lead us on to tackle a variety of challenges. It is a false pride that seeks to get by without asking advice. The experts are always available, an expert being a person who knows enough about a subject to be able to explain it lucidly to any intelligent questioner. Success depends on winning the goodwill and help of such people.

Each of us can learn as we work, and learn by our mistakes. Our capacity to learn by trial and error (the term for this being 'empiricism') has been one of the main planks of our evolutionary advance. Whoever was it who first discovered that chewing bitter willow bark could bring relief from aches and pains and reduce fever? It was a pioneering discovery that led, across many centuries, to the synthesizing of acetylsalicylic acid, or aspirin, which is still one of the most useful drugs in the modern pharmacopoeia.

Parents are naturally anxious for their children, and at this point they may well ask whether the sort of wide approach to everything which I advocate might not be full of dangers in the context of today's pressures and demands. Might they not lead to their children becoming jacks of all trades, masters of none – balls ricocheting aimlessly on the pin-table of life? It seems to me that the narrower approach has often had this very effect in the lives of children who drop out of the competition. A broader approach to the acquisition of all kinds of skills in the handling of people and materials may well equip them better for survival. They will be better prepared to make choices, and therefore to seize opportunities. All I can say, speaking from the viewpoint of my own case, is that I always found that no sooner had I mastered a job than it lost some of its fascination. In other words, I had succeeded; I was left looking around for the next challenge. In due course I turned my back on a 'secure' career in banking without having any idea of what other options existed for me. These turned out to be a set of risky tasks entailing film production, running a new television station and authorship. I found myself living a life that had nothing whatever about it of the routine or predictable. Instead, the fresh challenges came unheralded round the corner, usually on a daily basis. I would not have had it any other way.

As a producer or managing director, I never set out to place myself in the hot seat, responsible for everything that happened in any venture down to the last detail. But this was how it was, as it must be for anyone in a comparable position. The responsibility was overall, but the first discovery to be made was that you could not do everything yourself. You had to become, in the phrase I always used, 'a chairman of talents'. This meant gathering a team of the best possible talents about you, and surrounding it with a warm, encouraging, trusting atmosphere in which each member could enjoy the work they did and be aware of the real contribution they were making to the teamwork.

Another principle I followed as a managing supremo (and I would advise all others to do the same if they possibly can) was to join the relevant trade union. Masters and workers need to work in close harmony if they are to come up with the best product. The social division between management and shop floor has been a disastrous obstacle to progress through many generations in British industry – a waste of opportunities on an enormous and costly scale. In both the film and the television industries I always retained the trade-union membership which had been necessary to get me started in them. This meant that, whenever there was a strike – and there were plenty in those days, as often as not over demarcations of work duties – I would be down on the floor with the other members, eyeball to eyeball as their equal, and able to put my case. They, likewise, had immediate access to me, and most of our problems were solved on a basis of mutual interest before they could take hold in a general adoption of intransigent postures.

Jobs are created by customers requiring goods or services. Government may seek to intervene in the form of nationalization, minimum wage regulations and a variety of measures to protect staff. Unfortunately the effect of such well-meaning policies is to undermine the possibilities for successful new enterprises, with industrial ossification as the inevitable result. When no one can be fired, then overmanning becomes uncontrollable and the real cost of inefficiency falls on the shoulders of the hapless taxpayer. Inflation follows and formerly self-supporting families are forced to be reliant on welfare to live. In these circumstances, starting a new venture becomes simply too risky, except for those individuals or families who are bound together in their work by ties that are stronger than trade-union loyalties and can operate independently of such restrictions. The success of small individual restaurants, shops, farms and market gardens all depends on their being in the hands of people who welcome not having to observe set hours. Writers, artists and other individuals who 'paddle their own canoes' can work the hours they wish for as long as it suits them. Window cleaners, taxi drivers, gardeners, nannies and home helps all get by very well on an unrestricted basis.

Conditions for 'full employment' are not going to exist in the future, but since politicians require votes to enter and remain in government, it is natural for them to promise in opposition that they will bring about an end to unemployment if they are returned to power. It is easy to make such promises, but once they are in power they soon have to discover the reality that changes are made not by the Cabinet but by the leader. The Cabinet is a committee, and a committee's function is to present a range of informed advisory voices and views. The weakness of committees in decision-taking is that everyone wants their say to carry weight – hence the adage that 'a camel is a horse designed by a committee'. A fact continually confirmed by history is that world authority is in the hands of strong leaders, but their tendency to consolidate their power is mercifully tempered by the committees (cabinets, congresses, senates, parliaments) that back their leadership position. If this system ever ceases to work, then so does democracy itself.

For those who survived and endured a lifetime of work, the traditional reward used to be a marble clock for the mantelpiece. It marked an end to usefulness. Today we may say that education has failed us if all it inspires us to do is to choose to become boxed into lifetime commitments on the strength of the lures of apparent security – a terminal pension and a golden handshake, the metaphorical marble clocks for our age. Such perspectives and assumptions have become even more illusory than they were in the past. No matter how rich and eminent you grow to be before you step out of the work arena, 'The paths of glory lead but to the grave.' You only may arrive at the churchyard all the sooner, once your working umbilical cord has been severed by retirement and you have no more choices, hence no more opportunities. The one thing to be expected from a marble clock is that it will tick away till the last countdown. And this brings us naturally to retirement as the topic for the next chapter.

10

Retirement

Retirement was invented by the German chancellor Otto von Bismark when, in 1884, he inaugurated the world's first social-security pension system. It was he who arbitrarily set the age for retirement at sixty-five. Life expectancy at birth was then only some thirty-seven years. Today people are being induced to retire earlier, despite the fact that they are living very much longer. Job satisfaction is the best support for longevity, and early retirement may shorten the life-span, especially if it comes about as a consequence of redundancy.

In fact 'retirement' is the most disliked word in the whole of my vocabulary. It has the ring of a negative, unrewarding statement of defeat. It implies the giving up of a lifetime's work, of armies retreating to new positions, of ladies leaving the dinner table after the dessert, of people being put out to grass, of retirement homes – of God's ghastly departure lounges. The word needs to be removed from the language. People should simply change their occupation, and they should begin to lay their plans for this many years in advance.

Obviously people who genuinely love their work, or who cannot afford to take risks, should stay put, but it is a mistake to invest the whole purpose of your life in the institution which happens to employ you in whatever capacity it may be. This is to allow the organization utterly to define your status and dignity in the eyes of yourself, your family and your community. Herein lies a sure recipe for making yourself an early candidate for medical disaster as soon as that purpose is taken away from you. You need to acquire other interests long before you come within sight of your retirement date. These should be prospects that excite you and demonstrate that you are not merely an old horse turned out to end its days in grazing. Once the brain falls idle, it loses its sharp edge with alarming speed. To keep it young it needs new interests. Better to wear out than to rust up. The older we grow, the harder it becomes to make up for lost ground in the areas of physical and mental activity.

Pensions are not necessarily worth the effort. When I joined the Chartered Bank of India, Australia and China in 1924, I knew that retirement awaited me at the age of fifty. It seemed a wonderful prospect and a bargain, until I discovered that the average survival span of the bank's pensioners rarely saw them more than two years into their period of retirement. There were many who quite literally died within a few months of retiring. As I also observed, there were just a few pensioners who lived on into their eighties and nineties, but their longevity made the statistical expectancy of the others even briefer. Apart from these, there were also those who never reached retirement, but instead died in service from exotic diseases, misfortunes or the rigours of tropical climates.

I also witnessed those pensioners who came up to London from the country and called in at head office to chat to their old colleagues. Invariably the latter responded by asking them what on earth they thought they were doing, coming to visit the bank. Weren't they enjoying their retirement? But I could easily see how the boredom would set in for someone who found himself removed from a position of authority, enjoying power, servants, sunshine, sports and a lively social life, to, say, the misty Highlands of Scotland, where no one was going to be over-impressed by their yarns of the Far East. Such a dilemma never came about for me since I completed only sixteen years of service before I resigned. The reason for this was that the directors of the bank declined to grant me compassionate leave, at my own expense, to return home to be with my dying mother for the short time she had left. In the view of many of my colleagues, I had over-reacted by resigning. The fact that I had given up my title to pension and golden hand-shake seemed to them to belittle the jobs they were doing themselves. Yet it was a decision I was never to regret.

Professional people – members of the law or the medical profession, scientists, artists, writers, actors, entertainers, composers, sculptors, painters, academics, entrepreneurs, owners of businesses – retire, on the whole, when they choose. Many of them never retire completely at all. Instead, they nurture the hope to drop in harness. Even those who work for the security of a pension should, long before the time comes, develop hobbies and interests that will eventually keep them occupied rather than retired. They also need to bear in mind that there are certain activities which may not last as long as they do. Gardening, for example, presents an enjoyable option, but the time may well arrive when the physical exertion it demands is no longer possible and a garden that was formerly a manage-able joy becomes a nagging burden. Once again, it will pay to be adaptable and to fall back on concentrating on a less strenuous occupation that has been kept in reserve as a second string. Exciting alternative interests should be fostered early, and if they have a market or social value, and offer a degree of status within a community, then so much the better.

Therefore what to do? An adequate pension *is* important. It will provide freedom of choice during those later, potentially productive years. Today almost everyone has a right to a basic state pension, while extra state aid is also available to the needy elderly. It is already hard, however, to get by on these state-funded provisions alone, and it is going to be progressively harder in the future. As a result, there has been a tremendous burgeoning in private pension investment funds as a branch of the insurance industry, quite apart from other government-sponsored schemes. All of those in permanent employment pay some of their earnings into a pension fund, to which their employer also makes contributions, but the whole pensions field has become highly complex. It is possible to make a decision about transferring between pension schemes that you will come to regret, especially if you lack access to good-quality independent advice.

We may be sure that the speed at which the years leading up to retirement age pass will invariably catch us by surprise. Future pension provisions need to be closely monitored at regular intervals throughout this period. Like any other form of investment, individual schemes can vary considerably in terms of performance, yield and background charges. Factors such as values allowing for inflation also need to be taken into account, and every possible check should be made to ensure that a pension fund is properly secured. Those unfortunate pensioners who worked for companies owned by the late Robert Maxwell discovered the hard way how it is possible for supposedly inviolable funds to be vulnerable to business loss and fraud in the hands of an unscrupulous individual.

Such bad experiences should not deter us from making our own pension provisions. The picture is constantly changing. If you happen to switch your job, then make sure that your existing pension rights, or their true value, can be transferred to your new employment. If you are self-employed, then start to put money aside into a pension fund as early as possible in your working life. In the United Kingdom there are generous tax advantages for funding pensions of the self-employed, these rising on a sliding scale according to age. You always need to assess your own circumstances most carefully. Choosing a pensions adviser is as important as choosing a doctor.

Many pension schemes today involve provision for taking part of the benefits as a lump sum of capital, and it is important to decide how best to use this. When it came to retirement, some of my friends from the world of finance used a little of their pension capital to set up ethnic restaurants. They supplied English and banking expertise, while the Chinese, Italians, French, Thais and so on did the rest. Over the years I came to be astonished by how many people I knew who had developed connections with restaurants. One advantage, if there were no others, was that they could always be sure of a meal on the house.

Another friend, formerly a tea planter in Sri Lanka, retired to a dreamy village in Hampshire, where he had already bought his ideal cottage. In no time he grew tired of doing nothing, so asked his local bank manager whether there was anyone in need of help who could use his general experience. Before long he found himself caught up with a small local company making tubular farm gates and animal stalls. His organizational skills as a tea planter transferred easily and valuably to a small-scale industrial enterprise; the new venture turned out to be more profitable than his previous work. Since people take you at your own valuation, never underestimate yourself. There are always those whom you can help, and you don't have to be an expert in every field. Common sense and warm support are usually enough to carry the day.

With the retirement age constantly being brought down and life expectancy rising, most of us are likely to find at least twenty years available for the third stage of life. What are we going to do with this long stretch of time? The first priority is to make sure that it is enjoyable. At the age of sixty we have a rich accumulation of experience and are still at our mental best. It is no time to be giving up and grinding to a standstill. Potentially it represents the springboard for even more interesting and fulfilling ways of occupying our time on this planet. The fact that people are living longer must also mean that there is a market for secretaries and housekeepers for the elderly, so why live alone at great expense when it is possible to combine companionship, security and an income? Businesses must always need qualified temporary staff to allow their senior people to take holidays or to fill in for those absent through ill-health or maternity leave. And what about that pet project that we always had at the back of our mind, but could never clear the space to allow us to do something about it? At last it becomes a possibility. We are, to put it another way, left with no more excuses.

It is never too early to begin to consider the great variety of options that will be available once we reach retirement. At that point we become our own boss; at last it is our turn to pick and choose. We only need to take on commitments that we really want. I am convinced that it is possible for everyone to find a job or activity to bring them happiness, enjoyment and fulfilment at most stages of their lives, and that the last active stage may well yield the most golden opportunities of all.

As T. S. Eliot has written in 'East Coker', one of the set of poems that make up his *Four Quartets*:

Old men ought to be explorers
Here and there does not matter

SURVIVAL KIT

We must be still and still moving
Into another intensity

11

Death: The Yardstick for Living

The power behind religion, the largest and most lucrative industry in the world, is the fear of death. It helps to make belief in life after death irresistibly attractive: to see our loved ones again, to enjoy unlimited happiness, to be free of all emotional and physical pain, to live in paradise for ever.

The Pharaohs, the god-kings of Ancient Egypt, were among the first to take advantage of the fear of death for their own purposes of social control, and this lead was followed by later religions. The message was simple: there will be an eternity of suffering in store for you unless you allow your immortal soul to be saved by accepting belief in a specified form of religion. People divided by creeds have ever since fought opposing faiths for their right to eternity in wars that seem unending. Vast armament factories have prospered, and continue to prosper, on the backs of those who adopt religious conviction as an alibi for their personal tendencies towards ill-will and inhumanity. Religion, instead of binding people together in love and understanding, has both held them apart and driven them asunder.

Meanwhile religious orders and sects have grown rich and powerful on an endless flow of money subscribed to purchase a promise of eternal life. Facts may justify themselves in their own terms, but faith requires belief. Those who challenged belief in the past were killed and tortured, and even today few have the courage to challenge or question belief, even among the 'rational' peoples of the democratic West.

Recently even science has made its bid to get in on the immortality act. The alternative solution for attaining life after death which it has put forward is known by the newly coined term 'cryonics'. This derives from the Greek word kyros, meaning 'icy cold'. The idea is simple. A corpse is injected immediately after death with substances to preserve its cells from damage caused by the extreme cold (minus 196 degrees Centigrade) of the liquid hydrogen in which it is then to be suspended for a century or more. The theory is that this will give biotechnology the time to discover, at some point in the future, a method for reanimating the dead person, by which time the ills that caused the deterioration and termination of life will also be treatable. It is true that today human semen and eggs can be preserved for long periods by freezing, but these are single-cell suspensions and are not comparable with the complicated cell structures of the body – let alone the brain. The present cost for preserving a whole body in the United States is $120,000, with an annual subscription of $300 before death.

The attractions of the method are already making it a specialized branch of the mortician industry, with the element of faith being transferred from religion to technology. It blithely makes its claims without paying attention to the warnings against such exercises in human vanity with which the literature of myth has provided us. Tithonus, for instance, was granted the gift of eternal life by Apollo, but the boon of eternal youth was omitted from the deal. As a result it became the fate of Tithonus to age for ever into eternity, a dilemma hauntingly celebrated by Tennyson:

> The woods decay, the woods decay and fall,
> The vapours weep their burthen to the ground
> Man comes and tills the field and lies beneath,
> And after many a summer dies the swan.
> Me only cruel immortality
> Consumes: I wither slowly in thine arms,
> Here at the quiet limit of the world,
> A white-hair'd shadow roaming like a dream
> The ever-silent spaces of the East,
> Far-folded mists, and gleaming halls of morn.

My uncle William, the Belfast physician after whom I was named, would have regarded the notion of cryonics with scorn. He always said that he felt sorry for babies, coming into this world with all their troubles before them, and felt happier about the dying, who would shortly be free of further worry and pain. 'My last wishes are simple. No grave, no flowers rather donations to Help the Aged or similar charities. My ashes to be scattered on flowing water in the hope that one day their molecules will reach all the places in our beautiful planet which gave me so much happiness.'

In my youth, as I have said, the doctor's advice and wisdom were seldom questioned. Doctors enjoyed the complete trust of their patients. Disabled babies were not expected to survive to burden their parents with guilt and themselves with agonizing lives. The dying were similarly spared unnecessary suffering. These things are no longer such a simple issue. With the advances made in medical science, the acceptance of death has been lost, while the law requires that life be prolonged, even if the patient is suffering agonizing terminal disease and wishes to die. The medical profession meanwhile lives in anxiety of claims from dissatisfied patients or their relatives.

Euthanasia is legal in the Netherlands, and doctors in most countries do not allow their terminally ill patients to suffer unnecessarily, even though the large doses of pain-killers needed to relieve them may shorten their lives. There are certain doctors in these circumstances who, unfortunately for their patients, find themselves restricted in what they can do by a combination of their own religious convictions and the imposition of legal restrictions. Some healthy people in the United States of America, who are apprehensive that they may one day find themselves in such a situation, attempt to protect themselves by writing a 'living will' to document their wish to have their death managed with dignity in terminal circumstances. But such documents are not legally binding. The unfortunate fact of the matter is that euthanasia does open up avenues of misuse and that attempts to legislate to allow euthanasia will always be a potential minefield.

The original cause of death is birth. 'They give birth astride of a grave,' says Samuel Beckett's character Pozzo in a great play of the twentieth century, *Waiting for Godot*, echoing John Donne's seventeenth-century reflection that he was born in a winding sheet. The first thoughts of any would-be parents ought to be for the quality of life that awaits their proposed offspring. Circumstances may not necessarily be propitious for a baby in a world suffering from over-population. Some responsibility for this must be accepted by those governments and institutions which continue to encourage childbirth with religious and financial incentives.

Oddly enough, wild animals do not seem to have a fear of death. Stalked by a predator, they will continue to graze until the last moment, before bounding out of reach to continue to graze, apparently more concerned about eating than being eaten. Predators prey on the weak and unwary, agents for the natural law of the survival of the fittest. We feel sorry for an animal when we see it being struck down, but its time has come and our identification with its fate is an expression of anthropomorphism; we see it in terms of an individual event rather than as an episode in the history of a species.

On the question of survival after death, the French philosopher, Blaise Pascal, took the line of least resistance: 'Belief in God can make life easier. If there is no life after death, what have you lost?' Lord Wyatt expressed a more trenchant view when he was interviewed by Naim Attallah in *More of a Certain Age* (1993):

It all began with superstition and fear of the unknown. The idea of an afterlife seems to me to be inherently absurd; it's just sheer vanity on the part of man . . . I'm not in the least afraid of dying, though I'm annoyed that life is so damn short. I've wasted an awful lot of time by not working hard enough and now I feel 'Time's wingèd chariot hurrying near'.

Do we have any real reason to fear oblivion after death? Most of us seem to sleep at night undisturbed by the thought that we may never wake up, and death, as the saying goes, is the twin of sleep. I can only speak for myself in stating that none of the heavens on offer hold any appeal for me. The idea of eternity is one I find impossible to appreciate. Even a few hours' delay at the airport is an experience that seems interminable enough. Presumably my five senses and mind will cease to exist when my body dies, so if there is an afterlife, then the one thing about it of which I can be sure is that whatever is in store after death must be very different from how it was to experience being alive. Will it be fun? Will it be preferable to oblivion? Ah, indeed I wonder. The poet Stevie Smith once said: 'I really do think death will be marvellous . . . If it wasn't for death, I think you couldn't go on.' Her last poem was written in her hospital bed after a terminal illness had robbed her of the power of speech:

> I feel ill. What can the matter be?
> I'd ask God to have pity on me,
> But I turn to one I know, and say:
> Come, Death, and carry me away.
>
> Ah me, sweet Death, you are the only god
> Who comes as a servant when he is called, you know,
> Listen then to this sound which I make, it is sharp,
> Come Death. Do not be slow.

It is, as I said at the start, hardly possible that the enormous power which guides and regulates the universe could resemble us, though the original religious perceptions of *Homo sapiens* recognized its immense cyclical character. It has provided us with genes which cause the cells of our bodies to self-destruct as we move into old age. Ageing is a natural process which ensures that the next generation will be able to produce better people. The old stag is removed to make way for his strongest son, and thus nature improves the stock of the herd. The more we learn about nature, the less 'human' it seems to be in our terms. It has no consideration for the weak and helpless, yet it has given us the gift of living, albeit for a few brief years, on this splendid planet. Like Olympic runners, we have carried the flame of our unique set of genes through our own generation, in the midst of the millions of generations that preceded and come after us. We, the individual torches, burn out, but the flame is passed on. Perhaps this is where the real meaning of life lies: in the understanding of knowledge.

Death will end our world of the senses, but Mother Nature will waste nothing of us, even as she saw to the cycle of recreation for Thomas Hardy's vision of the lives of his 'Proud Songsters':

The thrushes sing as the sun is going,
And the finches whistle in ones and pairs,
And as it gets dark loud nightingales
    In bushes
Pipe as they can when April wears,
    As if all time was theirs.
These are brand new birds of twelve-months' growing,
Which a year ago, or less than twain,
No finches were, nor nightingales,
    Nor thrushes,
But only particles of grain,
    And earth, and air, and rain.

Our electrical components will continue their immortal lives and will regroup to make bodies for those who live in the future. Our days of life will not be forgotten; parts of us will survive death. The great men of history are better known today than they ever were during their lifetimes. Children and grandchildren and their descendants will carry our cells and genes into the centuries ahead, perhaps for as many generations as they have been handed down by our ancestors. The small ripples that spread out from our own impact on the journey through the ocean of life will touch shores more remote and distant than we can imagine.

Nothing is lost; nothing is wasted. Each of us leaves footprints in the sands of time. It seems arrogant within the grandeur of the whole vast design to demand a right to some sort of personal survival. The reality is the flame we have carried, which will continue as long as life exists. Our debt is to all those who have gone before and left us their enormous contributions for our welfare. Let us therefore try to leave in turn as great an inheritance as they did. The good we do to others is capable of outweighing any evil that may be done to us, and this should form the basis of our morality. It is for this reason that it is ultimately wrong to surrender to, or stand among, the ranks of the destroyers:

the men of ill-will who seek to impose their way on our planet with Kalashnikov rifles and Semtex.

In rounding off my thoughts on death it seems appropriate to quote what the great psychologist Carl Gustav Jung said in his famous 'Face to Face' television interview with John Freeman. Freeman had asked him: 'You have told us that we should regard death as being a goal and that to shrink away from it is to evade life and make life purposeless. What advice would you give to people in their later life to enable them to do this, when most of them in fact believe that death is the end of everything?' Jung replied:

I have treated many old people and it is interesting to watch what the unconscious is doing with the fact that it is apparently threatened with a complete end. It disregards it. Life behaves as if it were going on, and so I think it is better for an old person to live on, to look forward to the next day, as if he had to spend centuries, and then he lives properly. But when he is afraid, when he doesn't look forward, he looks back, he petrifies, he gets stiff, and he dies before his time, but when he is living on, looking forward to the great adventure that is ahead, then he lives; and that is about what the unconscious is intending to do. Of course, it is quite obvious that we're all going to die and this is the sad finale of everything, but nevertheless there is something in us that doesn't believe it apparently. But this is merely a fact, a psychological fact – it doesn't mean to me that it proves something. It is simply so. For instance I may not know why we need salt, but prefer to eat salt because you feel better; and so when you think in a certain way you may feel considerably better; and I think if you think along the lines of nature, then you think properly.

12

Summing Up

Humans need understanding to survive. Babies, after the shortest and most dangerous journey in the world, scream their needs with their first breath and fortunately are universally understood. As they grow up, their 'trailing clouds of glory' dwindle and they come to be divided by colour, nationality, religion, language and politics. Education and environment further reduce their natural freedom, but basic communication is still possible. Mime is international and simple. The need for food, drink, shelter or whatever is easily established. Nouns are also easy. Point to your chest and say your name, then point to the foreigner's chest, looking for an answer. After a few tries, he or she will respond. Finally they will tell you the name for any item at which you point. Before long, limited conversation will be possible, and even a joke or two may follow once basic understanding has been achieved.

Misunderstanding accounts for most of the violence in the world. Two world wars to end all war have led to the improvement of the killing machines but not to peace. The neutral nations interfere, but the only effect is to add fuel to the flames. As the proverb says: 'The road to hell is paved with good intentions.' The world has shrunk, however, and we are all neighbours; science has penetrated secrecy; there are no hiding places left. Massacres are watched as they happen. We are all responsible. The most powerful nation in the world, the United States of America, has recently come to realize the futility of trying to impose peace without the willing acceptance of those involved.

As a great philosopher of the twentieth century, Sir Karl Popper, has said, 'It is better that we trust our intuitions rather than abstract ideologies . . . The job of civilization is to make sure that we reduce violence.' Nikita S. Khrushchev admitted that the Soviet Union had 30,000 nuclear bombs, each of them many times more powerful than the Hiroshima bomb, and confessed in his memoirs that he had destined fifty of them for Cuba so that he might be able, in one stroke, to destroy the United States. Khrushchev is long gone, but what of those 30,000 bombs, and all the others manufactured subsequently? Who controls them today? What a temptation they must represent for cash-starved Russia, not to mention eager purchasers waiting in the wings. Surely the disposal of the planet's nuclear arsenals must be the free world's most urgent priority. Already the military of post-revolutionary Russia is giving signs of using its nuclear stockpiles to boost national pride with the most sinister and dangerous kind of 'sabre-rattling'.

Karl Popper has also warned us against the threat arising from any failure to see that questions of freedom and responsibility are utterly interdependent. 'There are great dangers in our world,' he wrote, 'among them the terrible idea that people must be able to do exactly what they like. Without responsibility there can be no freedom.' Today there is much educational emphasis on children having rights, but little indication of this being backed by ideas of service or duties. The results of teaching them to prize their liberties, privileges and entitlements, while leaving out of the equation the obligations and responsibilities which produce civil order, has been a rapid spread of aggression and lawlessness amid a proportion of young people.

In contrast to the human animal, which seems bent on self-destruction, the ants and the bees have happily solved the problem of living together in harmony within their own species. There are certainly various lessons that we can learn from the bee, that useful insect which has been around for more than 50 million years and is often held up as an example of excellence and diligence to the human race. Its approach to life is exact and successful – governed by the hive mind, a practical democracy. Even beekeepers are, like bees, servants to the hive. Despite prodigious efforts over the years, no way has been found to breed a bigger bee or to alter the pattern of community life or its natural cycle in man's favour.

Every hive is occupied by three kinds of bee, each born from one of the 3,000 eggs that the queen is capable of laying daily. It is therefore her awesome task to provide the hive's workforce of 60,000 worker bees to collect nectar during the season of the honey flow, and then to ensure that this force is reduced to 6,000 when the flow ceases and winter looms. This is the number that can survive on the winter stores, and the future of the species depends on the system working in this way. For *Homo sapiens* the world is overcrowded and the population is steadily growing out of control. Money talks, and if only some could be given to encourage families to have fewer children, then a real start might be made to addressing the basic problem.

Education may yet save us. By this I mean international education, which covers the world. No man is an island; we are one family; to know and to understand all is to forgive all. Education is daily becoming simpler and more attractive. Teaching machines, which will answer their questions, fascinate children, and 'computer speak' is already as natural to them as breathing. Entire encyclopaedias can be accommodated on a single 'CD Rom' disc, complete with animated teaching aids. Facts may thus be presented in ways that are imaginative and full of interest as well as being free from political bias. Such aids can expose the fruitlessness of 'winning' wars, gaining territory and exposing innocent people to death and starvation at the whim of some dictator or war-lord. The already ubiquitous nature of satellite television, and its rapid growth, will make it increasingly hard for sectarian despots to control the minds of citizens within the closed societies they would like to bring into being.

Thus there are hopeful signs. International trade and tourism are widely desired, especially by certain warring countries as they begin to see how they are losing out in global developments. They realize they can gain these prizes only if they are able to ensure secure and peaceful conditions for trading and visitors. Soon nations may have one universal language to run parallel with their national languages.

Children enjoy zoos, farms and seeing that milk comes from cows not bottles. No aspect of the way we live should be hidden. Lamb chops do not originally come wrapped in cellophane from a factory. The facts of battery farming, sewage disposal, mining, fishing fleets, hospitals, post mortems and the wonders of the human body are more important than animal parts hung up in butchers' shops. We in the West need to remember that a majority of the world's people are born and die in their own homes. It is a practice to which the more advanced countries may return.

Children are not frightened of death. In South Africa, in the Durban Reptile Park at feeding time, I watched as rock pythons were given pretty white live rats with sparkling pink eyes. Crowds of children leaned on the protective glass; mothers held up their babies to see. The rats were left to run about until suddenly caught and crushed in the enveloping folds of the reptiles; then they were slowly swallowed head first. I said to the keeper, 'But doesn't this frighten the children?' 'No,' he replied, 'they love it, and it makes them wary of snakes, as they have to be in this country. How else would you teach them?'

Many pupils are taught that the state is comprehensively responsible for their welfare, for seeing that they have work and providing for all their health care and future security. Clearly this is an impossible responsibility. In any case, there is more fun to be had from making your own way than in letting yourself be deprived of an exciting life by settling for a dubious security. The number of people starting up their own business is growing rapidly and the trend shows a high success rate. Government policies can fail on both the domestic and international level, and often do. The collapse of the Soviet Union provides an awesome warning, as, on a smaller scale, do failures among big businesses and banks in the free market area.

Knowledge comes from people as well as books. Everyone finds their own approach; no twin brains are the same, not even in identical twins. The brain is the powerhouse of our activities. Its billions of components never rest, but continually chart our way through life. Even in sleep, through the brain's activities at dream level, a great army of busy cells is helping us to consolidate the day just gone and to prepare us for the day ahead. Collectively they constitute the mind, the ghost in the machine, the still small voice. The answer to 'What to do?' rests between our own ears.

Important as it may be to fill our minds with people, books and travel – whatever transpires – the inner journey is even more important than the outer. It is our philosophy and vision that provides the sunshine or shadow for our lives, even as Blake saw 'heaven in a grain of sand'. We arrive on earth programmed by a million ancestors. Our parents, filled with love for us, continually tried to invest us with their approach to life. This may have reinforced our personal programming, or it may have sent it off on quite a different tangent. As a result, we may have found ourselves either harmonizing or at odds with our family. Some children take after their parents, others do not, and a measure of reaction against background is, in any case, a natural and healthy phase in the agonizing search for a stable identity that takes place during adolescence. This is an understandable situation, but success or tragedy may hinge on how the circumstances are handled, while a mutual sense of care and responsibility also needs to develop as a part of this interaction between parents and children. The young, too, must realize that this is a two-way process. 'Man, know thyself,' reads an inscription on a temple at Delphi.

First, therefore, we have to find ourselves, and after that it becomes clear that the most fundamental issue is for us to be true to ourselves while doing everything possible to remain aware of the views and feelings of others. Always be wary of accepting situations because everyone seems to do so without question. There would be no Christianity if Christ had simply accepted local custom.

So, in this day and age, what is the best advice we can give the young? It is certainly not to tell them to conform. Instead they should be encouraged to take their own course through school; to talk to their teachers about personal doubts, fears and longings; to learn first aid, typing and how to operate computers, which will help them to stay alive and record knowledge rapidly. The next priority for them, as they discover themselves, will be to develop the talents they possess and then move ahead on a basis of personal strength. It is better to be a happy trumpet player than a frustrated shipbuilder. They should never cease to whet their curiosity for the wonders of our world, for curiosity is the oldest and best teacher. They should listen with cautious scepticism to those who require them simply to mirror their own ideas, and stay close to those who share their enthusiasm for their own interests.

If there is family wealth that they may inherit, tell them to forget about it. It may lead them to depend on it for the future and come between them and the joy of living a creative life. If there is deprivation in the family background, they should beware of letting this become, in the same way, a continuing handicap that prevents them finding themselves. Many of the greatest people had humble and troubled beginnings, after all. They should also avoid 'isms' and political and religious movements which narrow the perspectives of their adherents. To paddle your own canoe is to enjoy your uniqueness.

> The world is so full of a number of things
> I am sure we should all be as happy as kings.

Actually, I rather doubt that kings are happy, but variety is the spice of life and the wider we spread our interests then the more we will enjoy life in the years we have to live. The prospects of exploration lie before the young, outwards from the community of home life, eventually to embrace the whole mind of our planet. The sooner they become familiar with nature's masterpiece, the greater will be the reward. As they discover where their real interests lie, the time also comes to discover the sort of work that will give personal satisfaction. Like a growing tree, the mind is in a constant state of change, and this is another factor to be used for advantage. The prospect of leading a happier and more rewarding life is more positively there than it can ever be for anyone who has a set and narrowed goal, and who, having devoted a single-minded lifetime to getting to a particular office in a particular block of offices, then realizes that he or she might have preferred another option. To survive in the realities of the world today, everyone needs to retain a maximum flexibility of attitude – to be creative and intuitive in the broadest meanings of these terms.

It is important never to be afraid to travel in one sense or another – to heed the urging voice. In his poem 'The Explorer' Kipling memorably conveyed that sense of excitement in an earlier colonial generation:

> Till a voice, as bad as Conscience, rang interminable
> changes
> On one everlasting Whisper day and night
> repeated – so:
> 'Something hidden. Go and find it. Go and look
> behind the ranges –
> 'Something lost behind the ranges. Lost and
> waiting for you. Go!'

There are, it is true, those who during their lifetimes seldom move more than a few miles from wherever they were born, yet who travel infinitely in their spirit and find wisdom and understanding. These are exceptional people. For most of us there are immense benefits to be had from physical travel across the world, as early in life as possible, on condition that we avoid the temptation to drag our own cultural baggage along with us and remain ever open to the cultures of others.

The best way for the young to see the world is always for them to work their way round it. Work puts us in touch with reality, with the real world. If they fetch up in a country doing work which they find congenial, then they should give it a go. If it turns out that, having chosen a job and country and applied their best efforts, they decide it is not really what they want to be doing, then they should not hesitate to change tack. In nature it is the animals which cannot adapt to change that perish.

Time is the most precious commodity in the world. There is no alternative to the principle of 'suck it and see'.

If we never wet out feet, we will never learn to swim. Trial and error and persistence have been the mainsprings for a rewarding life since the beginning of time. A 'safe job for life', even if such a thing exists, is likely to mean becoming a stereotyped 'company man', straining to maintain a position to secure a good pension, fearing the roulette of redundancy decisions, company takeovers or liquidations, hemmed in by equally nervous superiors. It means inhabiting a world in which office politics reign supreme, with all the stress and injustice that the phrase implies. On our own we either succeed or we fail, according to the worth that we have for society. There may be no company pension waiting for us, but neither will we have a boring retirement imposed before our potential has been used up and forcing us into an inactivity for which our working lives have ill-prepared us.

Since we live in the minds of other people, we need to set out to understand them. The one thing people are consistent about is doing what they consider to be best for themselves. Therefore we need to take an interest in their interests. Our greatest asset in life will be an ability to get others to help us, so we should always strengthen our relations with people – with any people. All have something to offer and most react to genuine warmth. Banish shyness. Ask about their work, their family, their country. There is often more wisdom to be discovered in a tramp than in a millionaire or company director; secretaries may well be more helpful than their bosses. Waiters and waitresses I have always found to be a friendly source of information. Many are away from their home countries; some are working their way through college. Hotel workers, policemen, railway staff – everyone enjoys talking to their fellow-humans. Bees and ants constantly relay information to their own kind as they go about their activities, and their organizational lifestyle has survived for more than 50 million years.

Do not worry over any fear of being a late starter or of

failing to arrive at knowing what you want to do. In my ninety-second year I have found that there are still so many options that I really don't know what I want to do next, though I remain quite clear about what I don't want to do. I was forty-five before I gave up my bachelor existence and, to my great good fortune, married Betty. Subsequently we have shared everything, especially the 'What to do?' decisions. One advantage of a happy family life is that you grow to be deeply concerned about one another and more able to tell those unwelcome truths that good friends might wish to side-step. Before I entered on to it I could never have hoped for the full and happy life that was to follow. Perhaps the most rewarding factor is that families contain a core of reality which sustains them through the difficult journey of life. Many of our projects and dreams have taken twenty or more years to mature, but we have always persisted. Nothing succeeds without persistence.

Religion, as we have seen, has an enormous influence over mankind, but the original teachings of love and respect for human beings have been manipulated by powerful organizations misusing their advantage. Believers, it is true, gain comfort, but the differences between religious sects (each claiming a metaphysical exclusiveness) continue to lead to intolerance, cruelty and devastating wars. 'Loving one's enemies' requires an almost superhuman generosity, but unless we develop sympathetic understanding for one another and the infinite number of roads that lead to the truth, then the human race must inevitably perish.

Will Rogers said, 'I never met a man I didn't like.' I feel rather the same about religions, and enjoy many aspects of them: the festivals, feasts, celebrations, music, chanting and singing, and all the attractions that go with Christmas, for instance. These beautiful and simple ceremonies have helped humanity and I hope they will long continue, but religious organizations have not brought about peace on earth; rather have they shattered it. The power that produced the universe and everything in it need not resemble us. It is an astonishing arrogance to assume that our perfection has been its ultimate aim. On 22 October 1994 *The Times* contained a report of a discovery of primate fossils in Aramis, Ethiopia. They dated back almost 4.5 million years, which meant they belonged close to the time when the evolutionary tree branched into two lines, one of which led to the apes, the other to man. 'This species,' said Professor Tim White of the University of California, 'is the oldest known in the evolutionary chain that connected us to our common ancestor with the living African apes.' Since humans and chimpanzees share 99 per cent of their genes, the implication is that the two species separated as recently as 6 million years ago. It is an implication that reverses the claims of religious orthodoxy that man emerged fully formed into being. It also strikingly supports Darwin's conclusions about the descent of man.

We are only one of a limitless number of possibilities among forms of intelligent life. The laws of nature apply to all creatures equally – popes and archbishops fare no better than the rest. Species are improved by the survival of the fittest, yet civilization protects the unfit. This ethical dilemma and contradiction represents the main challenge facing mankind today on our overcrowded planet.

Our beautiful earth is sinking beneath the weight of human pollution. It can therefore only be hoped that the time is near when religious orders, dictators and governments abandon attempts to encourage their peoples to have large families. 'Masses of evidence render the application of the concept of evolution to man and the other primates beyond serious dispute.' The fact that this statement originated from the Pontifical Academy of Science, and hence had received the approval of the largest established Christian Church, is a hopeful sign. It should give bigots pause to think again and ponder the laws of nature which govern all of us. Unfortunately, not all the signs are so encouraging.

The Times of 31 October 1992 reported that Pope John Paul II was rehabilitating Galileo, three and half centuries after the Inquisition of the Church of Rome held over his head the prospect of torture and death unless he recanted his discovery that the earth revolved around the sun and so could not be the centre of the universe. This in itself seemed a correct if long overdue move, but it also emerged that it had taken the special commission, set up in the modern scientific age to resolve the matter of Galileo's standing, thirteen years to arrive at such a conclusion! My preference is for the philosophy of the Irish poet James Stephens, who expressed the point that *really* matters with the utmost simplicity:

> No thought have I save that the moon is fair,
> And fair the sky, and God is everywhere.

From nature we receive our five senses and a brain carefully programmed to help us to survive and to think for ourselves. In addition, it seems, the enormous force that holds the universe in place may be tapped by some sixth sense which we possess in greater or lesser degree. My guru regarded the body as a projection of the mind, which is in control. Our unconscious minds or separate selves can be influenced by our conscious minds. Dr Emile Coué, an advocate of self-healing techniques, advised his many followers to use auto-suggestion. His famous device was the repetition of the phrase, 'Every day, and in every way, I am becoming better and better' – twenty times night and morning, using a knotted string or beads to avoid conscious thought.

Is there a yardstick for measuring life? Yes, there is, as we have seen, and a very useful one: death, our greatest fear in life. 'So teach us to number our days that we may apply our hearts unto wisdom' – Psalms 90:12. Self-preservation is our strongest instinct. The fact that we all have to die is certain. As Shakespeare wrote in *Cymbeline*, one of his late so-called 'winter' plays:

> Golden lads and girls all must,
> As chimney-sweepers, come to dust.

Pessimism provides a very good basis for a cheerful nature. If you don't expect much, then you won't be disappointed. But we can take advantage of the inevitable. People already do this by making wills and insuring their lives. We can also use it for decision-making. If I am not going to be alive next month, what ought I to be doing now? The answer is obvious: keeping in contact with friends and loved ones, 'grappling them to me with hoops of steel'. If one is ever going to say sorry, the time is now.

Death is a friend provided by nature to relieve us of all our grief, pain and suffering. It frames the picture of our life. Imagine the alternative – an unending sprawl across eternity. We should therefore come to terms with death, and this is more easily done if we have used it as a yardstick for living. Regrets at the end will not be for what has been done, even if our actions have at times been shameful, but for what we have left undone. The sins of omission will rankle more than the sins of commission.

Keep abreast of life, your affairs in order, your bags packed, your will made. Death should not be hidden. The more you talk about it, the less frightening it becomes. The aborigines of Australia have an ancient saying: 'The more you know the less you need.'

In my youth, it was thought to be natural for people to die, when the time came, in the comfort of their homes, surrounded by familiar things and, above all, by family and friends. Today, in Western society, they are more likely to die surrounded by strangers in nursing homes, or hospital wards. It therefore makes sense to try to arrange for a comfortable exit while you are still in charge, and to try to ensure you have it at home. The Chinese buy their coffins in advance of needing them. They pointed out to me that this had two advantages. For one thing, they obtained a better coffin; for another, they got it more cheaply.

So there you have it. Keep your body healthy, properly fed and exercised. Use your wonderful brain to the best of its abilities. Be true to yourself. And luck go with you. As Hilaire Belloc wrote:

> From quiet homes and first beginning,
> Out to the undiscovered ends,
> There's nothing worth the wear of winning,
> But laughter and the love of friends.

But let us leave the last word to the 'Song of the Harper', which speaks to us across the millennia from the wall of its Ancient Egyptian tomb:

Rejoice and let thy heart forget that day when they shall
    lay thee to rest.
Cast all sorrow behind thee, and bethink thee of joy until
    there come that day of reaching port in the land
    that loveth silence.
Follow thy desire as long as thou livest, put myrrh on thy
    head, clothe thee in fine linen.
Set singing and music before thy face.
Increase yet more the delights which thou hast, and let
    not thy heart grow faint. Follow thine inclination
    and thy profit. Do thy desires upon earth, and
    trouble not thine heart until that day of
    lamentation come to thee.
Spend a happy day and weary not thereof. Lo, none may
    take his goods with him, and none that hath gone
    may come again.

A Note on Physical Fitness

If you are resolved to take a positive attitude towards your health and well-being, and to prevent problems rather than treating them as and when they occur, then physical fitness must be an essential part of your life. Being fit has many advantages, from helping you to control your weight to giving you a better night's sleep. Most important of all, there is impressive and mounting evidence that people who exercise frequently, **and in the right way for them**, are less prone to such 'killer diseases' as heart attacks and strokes, and in fact live longer than people whose lifestyle is sedentary.

The Advantages of Exercise

* Reducing risk of heart and arterial disease and better control of blood pressure.
* More body flexibility.

* Weight loss in time (resulting from an improvement in dietary habits and a feeling of well-being).
* Better sleep (and sleep patterns).
* Pain relief (the correct kind of exercise will help pain such as backache, while menstrual pain in women can be reduced by exercise taken before and during a period).
* Simply better health all round (people who take exercise regularly have fewer days off sick).
* Relief from depression.
* Better performance at work and home.
* Improved concentration.
* Stress reduction.

The Risks of Exercise

Although the benefits outweigh the risks, there are nevertheless some risks associated with the taking of exercise. Incidences of injury vary with different sports and activities. They are low for **swimming**, but higher for activities involving **running**. The essence of avoiding injury is *to progress slowly.*

Good training shoes are essential for **jogging** to prevent injury to the **Achilles tendon** and the **knee** and **spine**. Always begin with **walking briskly**. Unless you intend to jog regularly, then continue with **walking briskly**. This will do you as much good as jogging.

Although the media will make headlines out of the news of a sports person dying in action, many, many more people die at home watching television than they do being active. If you already have a **heart condition** or **high blood pressure**, or any condition which requires medical advice, then be sure to have a check-up with your GP, who may even advise you to take some supervised exercise. Current thinking favours this approach.

As I have written on page 57, 'we will soon each carry a

136

computerized card containing our complete medical record, which will enable doctors, wherever we may be in the world, to diagnose and deal accurately with our medical problems as they arise'. Fortunately something of the kind was started for me nearly half a century ago by my employers, who insured all their employees with BUPA. I still get the computerized print-out of my annual health check. From this service it is only another step or so to a smart card. Many people dislike seeing their doctors, although they will readily take their car for its MOT test. Your body deserves more attention than your car. **Get to like it, learn how it works and how you can help to keep it well tuned.**

(Adapted from advice compiled by Kay Holdsworth, RSA, LAYH, Fitness Consultant)

Fortunately today, health insurance is a rapidly growing industry and the companies concerned realise that keeping their members well is better than paying hospital bills. Physical culture centres have become popular and the general health of the nation is improving.

(Adapted from advice compiled by Kay Holdsworth, RSA, LAYH, Fitness Consultant)

Career: William Baird MacQuitty

[Compiled by Peter Ford]

This colourful character, now in his ninety-second year, has been and remains, full of curiosity and a zest for living: he has always seized every opportunity to enjoy what he describes as 'the banquet of life'. He was born on 15 May 1905 in Belfast, his father being James MacQuitty, managing director of the *Belfast Telegraph*. He married Betty Bastin, economist, author, and a vice-chairman of Ulster Television. Their three children are Jonathan, Jane and Miranda. The many subjects in which he has taken an active interest over the years include anthropology, archaeology, bee-keeping, gardening, flying, underwater exploration, photography and a wide variety of athletics and sports.

Career

1924–39: banker in Belfast, London and the Far East. In 1926: special constable, City of London, during the General Strike. In 1927–32: served with Punjab Light Horse,

Amritsar. In 1928: founder member of the Lahore Flying Club.

1939: farmer, Ulster and the Isle of Man.

1939–40: diploma from the Institut für Psychotherapie under Dr Wilhelm Stekel.

1941–62: film producer and director. In 1951: founding director of London Independent Producers, productions including *Forbidden Cargo, The Prisoner, The Happy Family, Street Corner, The Beachcomber, Above Us the Waves*.

1914 to present day: photographer. His international photographic library contains 250,000 of his own pictures. Has had many exhibitions and examples of his work are in the National Portrait Gallery and the Imperial War Museum.

1965 to present day: author.

Films:

Produced 1940–46.

Wartime documentaries include *Simple Silage* (Ulster farmers' war effort); *A Letter from Ulster* (US troops arrive in Ulster); *Nineteen Metre Band* (BBC service to strengthen ties with India); *Out of Chaos* (Second World War seen through the eyes of famous artists, including Henry Moore, Stanley Spencer, Paul Nash and Graham Sutherland); *The Way We Live* (the citizens of Plymouth planning to rebuild their blitzed city). He also made the only film of T. S. Eliot reading his poem 'Little Gidding'; and filmed Stanley Spencer carrying out his crucifixion painting in Cookham churchyard.

Feature films, 1947–61.

Blue Scar (1948): Emrys Jones in a Welsh mining drama during nationalization.

The Happy Family (1952): Stanley Holloway in a Festival of Britain comedy.

Street Corner (1953): Peggy Cummins and Anne Crawford in a women police thriller.

The Beachcomber (1954): a version of Somerset Maugham's 'Vessel of Wrath', filmed in Sri Lanka with Robert Newton, Glynis Johns and Donald Sinden.

Above Us the Waves (1955): British X-craft attack on the *Tirpitz*, with John Mills, Donald Sinden and John Gregson. (It was Winston Churchill's favourite film).

The Black Tent (1956): the desert war in Libya, with Donald Sinden, Donald Pleasance and André Morell, script by Bryan Forbes from a book by Robin Maugham.

A Night to Remember (1958): classic account of the sinking of RMS *Titanic*, script by Eric Ambler from Walter Lord's book. Kenneth Moore heads a vast cast, but the ship is the star. Many awards, including the Christopher Award, the Golden Globe Award, the United States National Board of Review Citation, the Californian Motion Picture Certificate of Outstanding Merit, the *Picturegoer* Seal of Merit Award. The film revived public interest in this epic tragedy and led to the founding of '*Titanic* societies' around the world.

The Making of 'A Night to Remember': the producer's 1957 film of how the largest ship in the world was built and sunk at Pinewood Studios and in Ruislip reservoir. Its unique material features such famous survivors as Edith Russell, Lawrence Beasley and 4th Officer Joseph Boxhall.

The Informers (1963): a story about the Scotland Yard Ghost Squad, with Nigel Patrick, Colin Blakeley and Frank Finlay, adapted from Douglas Warner's novel, *Death of a Snout*.

Television:

1959–60: founding managing director of Ulster Television; 1960–75: vice-chairman. Originated the first adult education programme on television in the United Kingdom, *Midnight Oil*, a direct forerunner of the Open University.

Publications:

As author:

Abu Simbel (UK/US, 1965): includes the author's projected plan to save the temples by leaving them to be viewed from under water; it received international acclaim.

Buddha (UK/US, 1969), with a foreword by the Dalai Lama.

Tutankhamun, the Last Journey (UK/US, 1972): sold 250,000 copies and exhibition posters.

The World in Focus (UK/US, 1974), with a foreword by Arthur C. Clarke: a sampler of the world.

Island of Isis (UK/US, 1976): saving the temple of Philae from the rising waters of Lake Nasser.

The Wisdom of the Ancient Egyptians (UK/US, 1978), with a foreword by T. G. H. James: an anthology.

The Joy of Knowledge/Random House Encyclopedia (UK/US): major contributor.

Ramesses the Great, Master of the World (UK/US, 1979): saving his temples at Abu Simbel. (Film on the same theme, *Ozymandias: Ramesses the Great*, produced 1964.)

A Life to Remember (UK, 1991; paperback reprint, 1994) autobiography.

Survival Kit: How to Reach Ninety and Make the Most of It (UK, 1996).

As photographer:

Irish Gardens (1967), with text by Edward Hyams.

Great Botanical Gardens of the World (1969), with text by Edward Hyams.

Persia, the Immortal Kingdom (1971), with texts by Roman Girshman, Vladimir Minorski and Ramesh Sanghvi: commemorative book for the country's 2,500th anniversary.

Princes of Jade (1973), with a text by Edward Capon: the royal burial suits of Lieu Sheng and Tou Wan.

Inside China (1980), with a text by Malcolm MacDonald: portrait of the People's Republic of China.

Photographic archive:
The MacQuitty International Photographic Collection: consists of a library of 250,000 photographs taken by its founder over the past sixty years in seventy-five countries. Known and used world wide.

Awards:
Fellow of the Royal Geographical Society and the Royal Photographical Society.
Honorary Master of Arts, The Queen's University, Belfast.
Honorary doctorate, Occidental University of St Louis, Missouri.